M000105483

# OUT OF MY HEAD

*Coon dogs that lie to you,
killer pancakes, and
other lunacies*

## by LeRoy Powell

## Illustrations by Cal Warlick

PEACHTREE PUBLISHERS, LTD.
Atlanta, Georgia

Published by

Peachtree Publishers, Ltd.
494 Armour Circle, NE
Atlanta, Georgia 30324

Text copyright © 1990 by LeRoy Powell
Illustrations copyright © 1990 by Cal Warlick

All rights reserved.   No part of this book may be
reproduced in any form or by any means without the prior
written permission of the Publisher, excepting brief quotes used
inconnection with reviews, written specifically for inclusion in a
magazine or newspaper.

Manufactured in the United States of America

10 9 8 7 6 5 4 3 2 1

Design by Candace J. Magee
Cover illustration by Cal Warlick

Library of Congress Cataloging in Publication Data

Powell, LeRoy.
    Out of my  head : coon dogs that lie to you, killer pan-
cakes, and other lunacies / LeRoy Powell.
        p.      cm.
      ISBN 0-934601-95-X
      1.    United States—Popular culture—History—20th
century—Humor.
    I.    Title.
    E169.12.P685    1990
    973' .0207—dc20
89-28418
                                                        CIP

# Contents

**I suppose you're wondering...**

**ON THE ROAD TO SUCCESS** or
*If I'm So Smart Why Aren't You Rich?*

**WHEN I GET TO BE KING
THINGS WILL BE A WHOLE LOT BETTER** or
*Better Living through Lunacy*

**ANYTHING WORTH DOING
IS WORTH OVERDOING**

**THERE'S NO PLACE LIKE HOME...**
*Thank Goodness*

# *I suppose you're wondering. . .*

I do not want to brag, but I have the best job in the world. You might wonder what my job is. I think. The reason thinking is the best job in the world is that nobody can tell whether you are doing it or not. I have been practicing for a while, and I've gotten real good at this thinking business. I can even do it with my eyes closed. The only problem is that since folks can't tell if I'm doing it, they generally assume that I'm not, especially if they know me pretty well.

I could think a whole lot more if it weren't for the interruptions from people like my wife and my boss. I'll bet Albert Einstein or Thomas A. Edison or Leonardo da Vinci or any of those other great thinkers didn't have their wives and bosses bothering them all the time with trivial things like mowing the lawn or producing some visible results from all their thinking.

You may believe that I have a lot of nerve, comparing myself to Einstein, Edison, and da Vinci. Well, why not? We're all in the think business. The only difference between me and them is that they have already come up with great ideas, and I haven't. But I might break out with one at any moment.

I'm just going to close my eyes and get to work here............................zzzzzzzzzzzzzz.

# ON THE ROAD
## TO SUCCESS

*or*

*If I'm So Smart*
*Why Aren't*
*You Rich?*

# LAZY, SHIFTLESS AND WORTHLESS

If there is one group in this world that doesn't get any respect, it's the Lazy, Shiftless, and Worthless. Everybody is down on us, and I can't understand why. Here we are, not bothering anyone, and all we get is abuse.

It's the hard-working, ambitious guys that get all the glory. The eager beavers, the go getters. Your boss loves these people. Let him get a self-starting, goal oriented guy on the staff, and he really thinks he's got something. He does. He's got somebody who is out to get his job.

On the other hand, there's us shiftless bums. We do not eagerly beave. We do not go and get. Our only ambition is to make it until quitting time. We surely don't want to do our boss's job. We don't even want to do our own. You know the saying, "lead, follow, or get out of the way." We get out of the way. We are quiet, peace-loving people, not looking for recognition or fame.

Others do not realize the contributions we have made. As a matter of fact, all the progress in this world is the doing of the Lazy, Shiftless, and Worthless, because under our slothful exterior, there is a slothful interior. Ambitious people are crazy about working. We think working is crazy. We would rather spend our time thinking up ways to get out of it. That is the way we make our contribution to the betterment of the world. Who do you think invents all the labor-saving

3

devices?  People who like to labor?

All the way through history, it's been us, leading the way from a comfortable position.

Back in caveman days, the whole tribe would go out into the jungle to hunt carrying their primitive weapons, and they would surround and slay a mighty mastodon.  Now that right there is a lot of work, which you can understand if you have ever tried to beat an elephant to death with a stick. The cavemen were proud of their bounty, and they were looking forward to the barbecued mastodon supper that they were going to have back at the cave.  But first, they had to get the mastodon from where they had dispatched him to where the cave ladies were putting out the paper plates and fixing the potato salad for the picnic.  So there they were, happily dragging this hairy pachyderm through the bushes...except for the one lazy cave fellow who said to himself, "You know, if we put wheels under that thing, not only would we get him back to the barbecue quicker, but we'd have more energy for the square dance afterwards."

Skip forward a few thousand years. . .the children of Israel held in bondage and forced to build the great pyramids of Egypt. Imagine the labor of dragging blocks of stone weighing twenty tons across the sun-scorched desert for twenty miles. There was joy in their work too, as these people, held in slavery to the pharaoh, sweated and strained. Yes, the children of Israel knew that they were building more than a monument to a dead monarch, they were building a monument to themselves, too. A mighty structure that would last through the centuries as a memorial to their ordeal. This sustained them, and they were happy. As a matter of fact, most of them could hardly wait for the pharaoh to die so he could try the place on for size. And they worked on tirelessly except for one worthless Son of Israel who sat in the shade of a camel and said, "You know, if we had a D-6 Caterpillar tractor on this job, we could wrap up the Pyramid Project in a third of the time, build a first class parking lot and a four-lane access road and still come in under budget."

I am giving you these historical vignettes to illustrate what a debt we owe the Lazy, Shiftless, and Worthless. The backhoe was invented by a lazy ditch-digger. The elevator by a man who was so worthless he wouldn't walk up a flight of stairs. The digital wrist-watch was invented by a guy who was too sorry to figure out where Mickey Mouse's hands were supposed to be.

Do you see what I mean? You think working is hard? Ha! Try thinking. Once you figure out how to do things, doing them is easy. We lazy bums don't want the glory and respect of the world, but we would appreciate a little of its understanding.

Now you may want to ask me what wonderful contribution I have made to civilization. I haven't made any yet, but I'm liable to break out with a brilliant idea at any moment. Remember that the next time you see a Lazy, Shiftless, and Worthless guy leaning on a shovel. Don't harass him, he may be thinking.

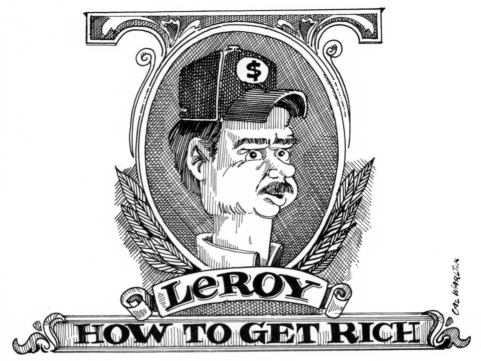

## HOW TO GET RICH

### EASY MONEY

How would you like to be rich? Rolling in money? With no risk and an investment of only pennies? I know it sounds crazy, but you can turn five cents into a fortune. It's true! And here is the best part. People will give you the money...for nothing. I am not making this up. I am also not asking you to send me money for the secret of this little bonanza. I am offering it to you for free.

Here's how it works. How do you feel about pennies? You don't want them, do you? Well, neither does anyone else. Pennies are genuine, American money, good hard cash, but most folks think they're a nuisance. They think pennies are only good for accumulating along with paper clips and pocket lint on top of

8

the chest of drawers.

If you drop a penny on the ground, most people won't even bend over to pick it up. This is the basis of the system that is going to make you rich. Now don't get the wrong idea. You do not have to go around picking up pennies off the ground—not unless you don't have any pennies to start with.

What you do is you get five pennies. Then you take these five pennies and go up to somebody and say, "Will you swap me five pennies for a nickel?" Now if they are like most people, they will tell you, "I will give you a nickel, but I don't want your pennies." Try this. It works! Folks don't want pennies so much that they will give their money away to keep from getting them.

Isn't this a grand idea? And all you have to do is take advantage of this pennyphobia to be on the way to your fortune. Just start out in the morning and go around all day offering people five pennies for a nickel, and at the end of the day, you'll have a whole pile of nickels and probably the same five pennies you started off with.

Now occasionally when you try this, somebody will actually take the pennies for the nickel. But if they do, you haven't lost anything. They've got your pennies, and you've got their nickel. All you have to do is get more pennies and start over again. There's no risk. And if you want to get rich twice as fast, offer ten pennies for a dime.

I want you to know this is not a get-rich-quick scheme. You've got to get out there with your pennies and work. But it is a plan that is limited only by your ambition and drive.

If you approach twenty people, you earn a dollar. If you approach two hundred people, you earn ten dollars. If you approach two million people, you earn ...however much two million times five pennies is. The size of your fortune depends entirely on you.

It's the American dream.  Success as the reward for hard work.  This only goes to show you that you don't have to be smart to get rich.  Some cents will do it.

# Picky Cars for Picky People

I know you are supposed to keep your mind out of the gutter, but when you're a jogger it isn't easy to do. The gutter is where you run, a never-never land between the traffic trying to run you down and the dogs trying to eat you up. So since you're out there in it you might as well think about it. The gutter, that is. Besides, if you don't look where you're going, you're liable to trip over something. The gutter is full of stuff. The more you look, the more you see. It's amazing. All sorts of things, just going to waste. There is a world of opportunity sitting right there on the side of the highway. Nuts, and bolts, and springs, and screws, and all sorts of car parts. Pieces of cars.

It seems like no sooner do the cars roll out of the factories, than they start to shed parts like dandruff. Some of them fall off, and some get knocked off when cars run into each other. And all you have to do is go along and pick all this stuff up. You may wonder why anybody with any sense would want to pick up a bunch of dirty, rusty, old nuts and bolts and headlight trim rings. It's simple. Let me ask you this. Doesn't your wife want a new car? Don't your children want a new car? Don't you want a new car?

Well, you can have that new car, and it's FREE! All you have to do is collect it out of the gutter. Every time you go out, just pick up a piece or two and stuff it in your pocket and take it home with you and put it in a box up on top of the chest of drawers next to all the pennies and lint and golf tees and business cards of people you don't know. Before you know it, you'll have such a pile of gearshift levers and sparkplugs and piston rods that you'll have to move it out into the garage, because your wife will tell you she's not going to spend another night in a bedroom that looks like a junkyard. When you accumulate enough pieces of a car, you can take them out in the driveway and get out your wrenches and pliers and start putting it together.

Some of the parts will be easy to come by, like the nuts and bolts, but some—like rear end housings and transmissions—will be hard to find. You may have to wait and watch the highway for years before you find just the right hubcap or oil pump or engine block. But sooner or later fate, reckless driving, and shoddy automotive workmanship will supply you with everything you need. Your new car is waiting for you on the side of the nearest highway. It will take patience and perseverance, but if you want a car bad enough, the opportunity is there.

It is very important to remember while you are collecting your car, not to become impatient. Do not pick up a whole car at one time. That is not nice. It is auto theft. Of course you should also remember that you don't have to make a car. I would like to have a truck. A pickup.

# SALESMEN

I admire salesmen. The best ones can sell you something you didn't know you needed and make you glad you bought it. Salesmen are what makes industry run because it doesn't matter how much stuff a factory makes, if somebody doesn't sell it, the company doesn't make any money.

A good salesman is fascinating to watch. He's like a sheep dog bringing in a stray lamb. His victim may not have any idea that he's about to buy something, but the salesman keeps on circling, cutting off every chance for the lamb to get away. Every time the lamb comes up with a new reason not to buy, the salesman is right there with two better reasons why he should. Finally the lamb has no other choice. He gets herded right up to the cash register and gets sheared. It's amazing. I am telling you this as a lamb of experience.

I don't know who the greatest salesman in the world was, that is, I don't know his name. But I have seen the evidence that he passed this way. He worked in Georgia about fifty or sixty years ago, around Greene and Hancock and Taliaferro counties. He sold lightning rods.

On every roof in the area over fifty years old stands the proof that he was the world's greatest lightning rod salesman. There is no more threat of lightning in Greene, Hancock, and Taliaferro counties than there is anywhere else, but you can't tell it by the lightning rods. There are enough lightning rods around there to protect every man, woman, and child in the area, and all of their pets, and most of their livestock. There are lightning rods by the dozens on the houses, and the barns, and the smokehouses, and the stables. Why a house should have six or seven lightning rods is beyond me, but they've got them. Just go look if you don't believe me. Where did they come from? From our hero.

He came down the road from one farm to the next, with a smile and a handshake and a model T Ford full of lightning rods. It wasn't just lightning rods he was selling. He was selling pride and protection.

All it took was the first sale. When he sold farmer Stringfellow one rod for his house, he had the key to the whole territory. The next farm he went to, he told farmer Armour, "Stringfellow over near Veasey is safe. How about you? Reckon you might be able to afford one rod?"

Well Armour was not going to let Stringfellow outdo him. If Stringfellow could afford one rod, Armour could afford two.

"As long as you're at it, Mr. Armour, it'd be a shame if your barn got hit."

Sold. With the Armour place sporting two new lightning rods on the house and one on the barn, the salesman went down the road to the Wooten place.

"Your neighbor Armour took care of both ends of his house, and you know, he even decided to protect his barn." Is Wooten going to sit still for Armour showing him up in the lightning rod department? No sir. Two rods for the house, and two for the barn, and one for the chicken coop.

Up and down the road the salesman went, hitting every farm in the area, pricking every farmer's pride, pitting neighbor against neighbor in the lightning rod race until he had worked them into a buying frenzy

and every house and outbuilding from Linton to Penfield fairly bristled with lightning rods; lightning rods festooning every eave and gable from Greshamville to Sharon.

Yes sir. That was a great salesman, and those lightning rods are still there today pointing heavenward, silent proof.

You may wonder what happened to this paragon of retailing. Did he take the fortune he made in Greene, Hancock, and Taliaferro and retire? I don't know, but I doubt it. True salesmen never retire. Did he move on to a new territory? I don't think so. There are no other areas around here with the same concentration of lightning rods.

The way I figure it, after his merchandising triumph the salesman planned on conquering new territory, but before he could, he had to restock. He was completely out of lightning rods. He telegraphed the factory, and in a couple of weeks, he went to the railroad depot in Greensboro where waiting for him was a boxcar load of shiny new lightning rods.

He loaded them in his car until the Model T couldn't hold any more, and then he bought a trailer and loaded it too. Off he went through the countryside, with a song in his heart and the prospect of all of Georgia made prickly as a porcupine with lightning rods.

In this happy state of mind, the salesman didn't notice the clouds beginning to gather in the summer afternoon. From miles away they drifted together, as if drawn by some mysterious magnet. All these clouds merged, uniting in an enormous thunderhead that floated ominously, directly above the lightning rod-laden Model T.

He was headed for Maxeys just across the Oglethorpe County line when it happened. There was one gigantic supercharged bolt of lightning. Nobody ever saw that salesman again.

I don't know if that's what happened, but you'd think he'd want it that way.

That is not the end of this story. A few years ago, evidence surfaced that our salesman has kin in Florida. It was a news story out of Jacksonville that reported the sale to a tourist attraction in Israel of 122 alligators.

A tourist attraction doesn't need 122 alligators. All you need is two or three alligators and 122 billboards to put out along the highway saying, "SEE LIVE

ALLIGATORS!" You can also put out some signs advertising guava jelly and souvenirs. That's the way they used to do it on U.S. Highway 41 in South Georgia, and it seemed to work just fine there. It ought to work in Israel, too.

So how does a Florida alligator salesman go about selling 122 alligators to the Israelis? These people are not known for making stupid business decisions. They know full well that a couple of gators will do the trick, but they also know a bargain when they see one. That's why there are 122 alligators. When you buy ten dozen alligators, they throw in two alligators for free. That's salesmanship.

# To the Pointe

How would you like to earn a million dollars in real estate? All you need is a good name. Not the name that your mama and daddy call you, the name you call your real estate. I have been thinking about this because of all the developments going up named something-or-other pointe.

Pointe is French for what ballet dancers do when they're dancing up on their tippy-toes. They're "en pointe." Now do you believe that all those real estate developments are trying to appeal to the ballet dancing trade? Of course not. They hang that "e" on the end of "point" to make it sound like their particular office park or condominium has a bunch of class. That way they can charge more for it.

You may wonder how to turn your particular hunk of land into valuable investment property. Just give it a good name. You don't even have to think of a name. You can pull one out of a barrel. Trust me.

First, get a barrel. A nail keg will do. Then get a bunch of pieces of paper, and on each piece, write a real estate word.

Put some tree names in first. Oak, Elm, Poplar, Maple, Cedar, Spruce, and Pine are good ones. You can't go wrong with tree names. Don't worry about whether there are actually any of these kinds of trees in your development. You will probably want to bulldoze them anyhow.

Now that you have your tree collection, put a few

animal names in the barrel with them. This is a little trickier than trees, because there are good real estate animals and bad real estate animals. Fox, Deer, and Eagle are good; Possum, Weasel, and Skunk are bad. Do not include any bad animals if you want to make good money.

The same goes for geographical features. You want to have some good sounding topography. Lake sells. Swamp doesn't. Throw Hill in the barrel, and River, and Valley, and Forest, and Meadow. Put Canyon in, leave Gully out.

There are all sorts of things that you can include. Italian and French words are good. So are English place names, except for Liverpool and Bath. German and Russian words are iffy. Flowers can be good, especially Rose and Lily. Vegetables, on the other hand, are not going to raise your land value. Nobody is going to put their money in any place named for Cabbage or Tomato.

The last things you write down and put in your barrel are purely real estate words. They don't mean anything about real estate, but they sound good. Words like Chase, and Hunt, and Run, and of course, Pointe.

By this time you should have a barrelful of slips of paper with names on them. Now you stir them well until they're all mixed together, and you're ready. All that you need to name your development is in the barrel. Just reach in and start pulling out words.

Don't worry that you might pull out some words that won't go together. They all go together. Even if you get two from the same category, they still make dandy real estate names. You don't believe me? How does Spruce Pine sound? How about Chase Pointe? You can't go wrong with this. Even if you pull two opposites, it doesn't matter. Summit Valley works.

21

They all do. Any two pieces of paper you pull out of the barrel will be a perfect name for your apartment complex or subdivision. If you want, you can pull out three words. Deer Hill Canyon. It still does the trick.

All this time you may have thought that it takes hard work and perseverance to make it big in real estate. All it takes is a good name. It says in the Bible that a good name is rather to be had than great riches. In real estate, a good name will get you great riches. Your fortune is there, in the barrel, waiting for you. Like I said, real estate names don't have to make sense. All they have to make is money. Get my pointe?

# HOLD IT

Have you ever wondered how the boss gets to be the boss and you don't?

After all, you probably work four or five times harder than he does, and you are probably just as dumb as he is. But there you are, slaving away, and there he is, doing nothing and getting all the credit. It doesn't seem fair, does it?

You have got to figure there is some reason for that, so try this for an answer. Notice the boss when

23

he's standing around like he does most of the time. Notice his hands. He's got ahold of something, doesn't he? Well, that's it. The one in charge carries something around with him to make him look like he's doing something when he isn't. Now here's the important part. Whatever he carries around can't be something that he can do any work with. Do not make the mistake of lugging a shovel around, or somebody will expect you to dig some ditches. You've got to tote something useless.

Just think about this. Think about people who are in charge of things. Think about kings. Kings are world champions at doing nothing, and they've got whole countries to do it in. Kings carry scepters, and they get to sit around all day on their thrones while everybody else in the country is working for them.

And generals. How about generals in the army? They carry swagger sticks. You would have to be nuts to take a swagger stick out on the battlefield and try to fight somebody with it. But generals don't have to fight. They've got all those soldiers to do it for them. And when the battle is won, who gets the credit for it? Right. The general, who has done nothing but wander around holding a stick. Does this sound like where you work, or what?

It's a symbol of power. Your boss may only carry a clipboard, or a pencil, or a telephone, but if he's the boss, he's got to hold something. To get to be the boss, you have to look like a boss. Stand around with a hammer in your hands and folks will think you're a carpenter. Stand around with your hands in your pocket and folks will think you're a bum. But stand around with a stick in your hands, and people will think you're in charge.

Don't try to thank me for this insight. I'm happy to help.

# WHEN I GET TO BE KING THINGS WILL BE A WHOLE LOT BETTER

## or

### Better Living Through Lunacy

# PROBLEMS

I would like to discuss the biggest problem in the world. It may come as a surprise to the people who know me that I know anything at all about things like that. They all think the only problem I know anything at all about is how to get out of work so I can sneak off and go fishing. But I know what the biggest problem in the world is. The biggest problem...is yours.

You may be wondering what the fool is talking about. I am talking about your problems. Yours. When something is bothering you, it's more important to you than anything else.

Take underwear. Have you ever been getting ready for church and when you rooted around to the bottom of the chest of drawers, you found out that you only have one set of didies left...and it's those shorts that are all raggedy and full of holes that you were going to chunk in the rag pile the next time you got around to it. But it's all the underwear you've got. So you go ahead and put them on because it's time to go to church, and for a change your wife is hollering for you to hurry up and get dressed.

So there you are in the sanctuary, and when it's sermon time, the preacher may be giving sin down in the country, but back in the back pews, you're not worried about sin. You are worried about eternity. Eternity is sitting through a church service with raggedy underwear thinking about being in a wreck on the way home...imagining yourself battered and bleeding

in the mangled wreckage.  The ambulance comes and
speeds you off to the emergency room at the hospital,
where the doctors and nurses rushing to your aid heap
ridicule upon you when they find out you are wearing
raggedy underwear.  And after your mother warned
you about just that very thing.

Or how about being seasick? Imagine yourself floating along in a boat on the ocean, and the boat is going uuUUUUPPP ANd down, uuUUUUPPP ANd down, and so is your stomach. Some people never get seasick. That immunity makes them mean. They may be your best buddy on dry, stationary land. But let them be along when you are draped over the side of the boat, contributing everything you have eaten for the last month to the fish, and they'll offer you a greasy sausage biscuit and laugh about it.

There you are, sicker than a pack of dogs, and you have just found out your best buddy is a sadist. The last thing on your mind is the rate of unemployment, or the plight of the homeless, or the depletion of the ozone layer, or the threat of nuclear war. You would welcome nuclear war, if they would only start it directly on top of you right now. All you want to do is return to solid ground, where you can quietly die lying still. . . right after you murder your buddy.

If you are not afflicted with these problems right now, you may not think they are very important. But slam the car door on your thumb, and it will take your mind right off inflation or any other external problem you can name.

I am not saying that the problems of the world are not something we should think about. But before we can solve the world's predicaments, we have to deal with the problems inside ourselves. The biggest problems in the world aren't out there. They're in here. Ask a man with a toothache.

# NEW YEAR'S RESOLUTIONS

Children are a lot smarter than grownups. Children will be good just before Christmas so Santa Claus will bring them a bunch of gifts. Grownups, on the other hand, will wait until New Year's Day to resolve to be good, and for no particular reason.

New Year's Day is for football games, black-eyed peas and hog jowl, hangovers, and resolutions. Lots of times it's the hangover that causes the resolution. Countless amateur drinkers who ran wild on New Year's Eve wake up January first with heads that feel like a beachball full of killer bees and mouths that taste like the Augean stables, and they swear never again will they touch liquor.

As a veteran at repentance, may I offer a couple of pieces of advice in the resolution department. Number one: Never make a resolution to quit drinking when you're on a hangover. As sincere as you are at the time that you'll be a sober and upright citizen for the rest of your life, you know deep inside you don't mean it. You are being held under duress by your body, and you will tell it any lie to make things better. Contracts made under coercion aren't binding, and neither are resolutions.

Number two: If you are going to make resolutions, have them prepared and handy before New Year's Day. This will give you time to plan and consider all of your evils and judge which ones you are sort of fond of and which ones you can do without. This way you have a better chance of actually living up to your resolution all the way through January.

I personally have given up rutabagas.

"Aha!" you say, "He doesn't like rutabagas anyhow."

Wrong. I don't love rutabagas, but I don't have anything against them either. When it comes to rutabagas I am absolutely neutral. That's what makes them a perfect object of my personal resolve.

It's not honest to give up something if you don't like it in the first place, because you don't get any moral satisfaction out of it. If, for instance, you can't stand liver, resolving not to eat liver won't make you feel like you have improved yourself. You probably wouldn't eat liver anyway.

The same thing goes for giving up things like jumping out of airplanes without a parachute. You've got to start doing something before you can stop.

But something you are indifferent about is different. Take rutabagas in my case. I have eaten rutabagas in the past and liked them just fine. So I feel like it is honest to give up rutabagas. It is also something that I am tested on every once in a while. Occasionally I'll find myself in a cafeteria line or at a dinner on the grounds and there in front of me will be a bowl heaped up with rutabagas, all orange and steaming. I even get a twinge of temptation to try a bite or two, but thanks to moral strength and the fact that the twinge isn't strong enough to work up into a real rutabaga craving, I can resist the urge and move along to the fried chicken a better man.

The first year I gave up rutabagas was 1972. It has been my resolution every year since then. In all those years, rutabagas have not passed these lips.

It is a great credit to humanity that we, of all creatures, are the only ones who try to be better than we

31

are.  When it comes to making New Year's resolutions, choosing ones that are easy has two advantages.  First, if you make a resolution that you actually keep, it makes you feel morally superior to all those poor weak souls who fall by the wayside in only a few days or weeks or months.  And second, if you start out by giving up the easy stuff, you can work your way up to things that are harder.

I personally am considering giving up egg drop soup next year.

# LIFE IN THE SLOW LANE

Some people are meant to go through life in the slow lane, and I'm one of them. This is the sort of thing that you figure out after long and bitter experience. Goodness knows I've spent enough time trying to be a fast lane person, but you are what you are. I finally got this fabulous insight at the grocery store. In the checkout line.

The only time my wife will let me go to the grocery store by myself is when she's out of something. She gives me the list for a loaf of bread, a dozen eggs, and a bag of onions. That is all she wants, just those three things.

Now I feel that if you're going to do something, you should do it with flair and style, and going to the grocery store for three things is a waste of time. This is especially true if you're going for three ordinary items like bread, eggs, and onions. I think if you are going to use your time and energy to go shopping, the least you can do is come home with some interesting stuff in your grocery sack.

So there I was, with a pound and a half of Swedish havarti cheese, a gallon of pecan praline ice cream, three cans of sardines, two boxes of snack crackers, and a bunch of grapes. As I approached the checkout line, I carefully studied the situation to plan my strategy.

There were five people in the express checkout lane. In the next lane seven people were lined up, their

33

carts piled high with a month's supply of groceries.
Then there were two closed lanes, and an open one
with two patrons in the line. One was a young mother
with a cart half full of groceries and half full of a baby
in the seat thingie.  The other customer, the one in
front, was a nice old lady with just a few things in her
cart.

Quickly I surveyed the scene and shrewdly chose
to join the last line—the one with two people.

The nice elderly lady had coupons. Lots of them. She had to sift through them to find the ones that matched what she was buying. Meanwhile, the other two lines were moving like lightning. I was determined to stick with my first choice, until the cashier came upon a half carton of eggs in the old lady's cart. "You can't buy a half dozen eggs, ma'am," explains the cashier. "I don't need a dozen eggs," rejoins the lady.

I missed the rest of the discussion as I moved to the express lane, which by then had grown to six people.

Things were going great in my new line. The cashier's fingers nimbly danced over the cash register. She finished the first cart. The customer wanted to pay by check. The check was drawn on a bank in British Columbia. I noticed the line next door had dwindled to one weekly shopper, and she was just about finished. I moved to that line as the cashier informed me, "Sorry, I'm about to go on break."

Only two lines now to choose from. In the express lane, negotiations continued over the Canadian check, but in the other lane, the old lady and the cashier had settled their differences and amicably parted, leaving only the young mother, and two new customers with medium full carts. I go back to lane number one.

It was there that insight struck. Just as the young mother discovered she had a bunch of items in her grocery cart that she hadn't put there, but her baby had, it came to me. It's all my fault.

Every time I get in a line, the line stops. If I change lines, that new line stops. Clearly, I have strange powers far below those of mortal man. Slowman! I have this aura about me that influences people ahead of me in line. It's not their fault, it's mine!

I am the one at the K-Mart who makes the price tags fall off items, so the cashier has to holler to the back of the store for somebody to find out what they cost. I am the one who gives the lady at the front of the line at the bank an overwhelming urge to discuss her grandchildren with the teller. I am the one who always chooses the lane of traffic on the interstate that immediately grinds to a halt.

The world hurtles by with all its adventures, and here, aching to join it am I, stuck in the slow lane. And I forgot the eggs, bread, and onions too.

# METRIC TIME

You want to go out to the lake and aggravate the fish. Your wife wants you to fire up the lawn mower and attack the rising jungle you have allowed to grow out there in the yard. Your boss wants you show up early, stay late, and be productive, doing whatever it is you do at the place you work. Do you have a hard time fitting all of this into 24 hours? Well, everybody does. Folks are all the time complaining that there just aren't enough hours in a day. So why don't we do something about it?

I think we need to start using metric time.

Most of the rest of the world is already on the metric system, and in this country we're getting more and more of it. Most track meets these days have the races in meters and kilometers instead of miles and yards, and the nuts and bolts on your car are probably metric. They even sell Coca-Cola in liter bottles. So, since they've got metric everything else, why not metric time?

You see, the metric system is based on tens and hundreds and thousands, so metric time would work that way too. You'd have 100 hours in a day and ten days in a week and so on. (If a hundred hours in a day isn't enough, you're just too busy.) With a ten-day week, you would still spend five days at work, but you'd have five more days to look forward to every weekend. So you could spend a whole day doing all

37

the stuff your wife has been after you to do around the house and still have four days for important things like fishing and hanging around the Army surplus store and watching ball games on the TV and sleeping on the sofa and things like that. Does this begin to sound good?

Of course, in the metric system, you have to have a basic unit to measure by. They use liters for volume, and meters for distance, and grams for weight. Metric time would have to have something like that too. You can't use minute or second or year, because we already use them to measure Fahrenheit time, and it would be confusing to use them for the new system too. Some people would probably like to make up a new word to measure metric time, but we've already got lots of words about time that don't have any specific meaning; words like moment, and flash, and age, and eon. Why not use one of them? Now a moment and a flash are too short for your basic time, and an age and an eon are too long. I like a nice medium time word. I like littlewhile.

Think about it. One hundred littlewhiles in a day, and a thousand millilittlewhiles in a littlewhile. A metric week would be a kilolittlewhile. Isn't that elegant?

Imagine how easy it would be for children to learn to tell time with nice, neat tens and hundreds and thousands to deal with on the clock instead of all those sixties and twelves and twenty-fours they have to try to figure out now. And no more, "Thirty days hath September, April, June, and November." One hundred centilittlewhiles hath September, and all the rest of the ten months in the metric year. I realize that we are going to have to drop a couple of months to get it down to ten. I nominate January and February. They're both too cold anyhow.

How grand it would be. How simple. It's time we abandoned the clumsy system we've been stuck with for all these years...excuse me, megalittlewhiles. I believe this deserves more study, which I plan to give it...in a littlewhile.

CAL WARLICK

## SAVING DAYLIGHT TIME

Daylight-Saving Time is a wonderful idea. All summer when the days are long anyway, you've got the clock set forward an hour, so you have an hour's extra sunshine in the evening to play golf or go fishing or work in the garden. You may have a little trouble getting the children off to bed when it's still daylight outside, but since it's school vacation, that's not a huge problem.

The problem comes when you go back to Standard Time in the fall. Instead of having an extra hour of light to play with in the evening, you have an extra hour of morning light. This is fine for getting the kids off to catch the school bus, but since the sun goes down an hour earlier, those of us who work have to come home after dark.

It makes sense to have Daylight-Saving Time, but

Standard Time just doesn't get the job done, clock-wise. What we're doing here is forcing something on nature that doesn't have any relation to reality. You know that the days are getting shorter, but your clock doesn't. It just keeps ticking away like there are twelve hours of daylight every day, and twelve hours of night, no matter what time of year it is.

What we need to do is get in tune with nature. I have been thinking about this, and I think I've figured out how to do it.

Since the days in winter are short and the nights are long, what we need to do is adjust time to fit that arrangement. With Daylight-Saving Time, we make the days of summer longer. In the winter, we need Saving Daylight Time. This would make time shorter in the day, and longer at night. Now pay attention.

We want daylight in the morning for the sake of the school-bound tiny tots, and we want daylight in the evening for us big tots, but nature has made the days shorter. The solution is for us to take an hour out of the middle of the day and slide time in from both sides.

I nominate the hour between eleven a.m. and noon. Nobody would miss that one. All you do then is wait for lunch anyway, and with that hour gone, you wouldn't have to wait. Isn't that nice? You could slide right from coffee break to lunch hour with almost no annoying work to distract you. So now we have made the day shorter, but we haven't lost any daylight. We've gained some because when we bring the hours of ten and twelve together, we drag more sunlight into the morning and evening ends of the day. Now we have a shorter day with more sunlight.

We also have this extra hour waving around loose. We use that hour to make the night longer. The night is supposed to be long in winter. That is the way nature intended. I suggest we slide the spare hour in between two and three o'clock in the morning. Everybody is asleep then, and with a spare hour in there, you get an extra hour of sleep every night. Is anybody going to complain about that? Of course not.

This is brilliant even if I do say so myself. What we have done is make from six in the morning to six in the evening eleven hours long and from six in the evening to six in the morning thirteen hours long. And eleven plus thirteen equals twenty four hours in a day and everything comes out right, right?

It is simple and elegant. The kids get to go to school in daylight, and you get to come home in daylight. Lunch comes an hour sooner, and you get an hour more to snooze every night. And the best part is, we have done all of this while bringing time and nature into harmony with each other.

Sometimes I'm so smart it scares me.

**SNARF**

I have been wondering whatever happened to the interrobang. You may not remember it at all. The interrobang is a punctuation mark that somebody thought up fifteen or twenty years ago. It looks like what you'd get if you crossed a question mark with an exclamation point. This is an interrobang: "‽"

Actually, a cross between a question mark and an exclamation point is exactly what it is. It is punctuation to show that whoever is talking is excited when he asks a question. "The doctor says you're what‽"Now that is an interrobang sentence. It would be good for the sort of situation where a question mark doesn't show the emotion you want, and the exclamation mark doesn't show that it's a question. The interrobang says it all.

Well, the interrobang never caught on, and I don't

understand why. We have got a blue zillion words for making sentences, but only three punctuation marks for ending them—the period, the exclamation point, and the question mark. If we want people to know exactly what we're trying to tell them, we need the interrobang. I think we need the wimpersand and the snarf, too.

I just invented the wimpersand and snarf. The wimpersand, also known as the whine sign, looks like this: " ⸮ " It is used for all those situations where you need to end your sentence with a wimpy sort of whine. Notice this example. "Mom, Johnny keeps calling me naaaammmes ⸮" Compare it to the way we've had to do it up until now. "Mom, Johnny keeps calling me names." Now you tell me which one does the job better.

My other invention is the snarf: ⟨⟨⟩⟩ You use this one when you're angry. "Learn how to drive, you b.b.-brained baboon⟨⟨⟩⟩" This is a lot better than using an exclamation point. In this sentence, you do not want to show that you are excited, you want to show that you are turning purple and there is steam coming out of your collar and smoke out of your ears.

Just imagine the creative vistas you can open up with the interrobang and the wimpersand and the snarf. Suddenly it's easier to say what you want to say and know what others are saying. Imagine getting a note from the boss, "See me." This is cryptic. You don't have any idea what kind of situation you're walking in on. The boss might be getting ready to fire you, or he might be getting ready to give you a raise. But if he writes, "See me⟨⟨⟩⟩" you know. You don't even have to bother seeing him. Just go ahead and clean out your desk and head for the door.

If you think the wimpersand and snarf are good by themselves, wait until you start combining them. Just as the interrobang merges the meanings of question mark and exclamation point to get a separate and different meaning, you can cross the wimpersand and snarf with other punctuation to get the exact shade of emotion that you're looking for. For the more than merely angry, try a snarfbang⸮. For the question that is whiney and annoying, use an interrowimp ⸮ . And for the angry, excited, wimp, the wimpsnarfbang. "You painted my cat purple, and I'm telllinnnnng⸮"

In a world where communication is so important, I am surprised that the interrobang has yet to gain wide use, and I'm amazed that nobody else has come up with the wimpersand and the snarf. I offer them to you. I modestly take credit. If it's O.K. with everybody⸮

# SITTING

Now that they don't build houses with front porches off the ground anymore, do you ever wonder what old hound dogs do for relaxation? There is no scene of tranquility so vivid as a hound dog under the porch with his face between his feet, blowing up little dust clouds every time he breathes out. The only thing close to it is the people up on the porch, sitting. Sitting is an art that isn't getting passed along.

People these days feel like they have to be doing something. If they're not working, they're jogging, or playing tennis or golf, or taking courses to improve their minds and bodies—or they're parked in front of the TV set. Sitting in front of the TV set isn't sitting, it's watching.

People used to sit a whole lot. You'd walk down the street or drive down the road, and there they'd be, out on the porch, sitting. The porch wasn't the only place. Folks had a choice of sitting places. You could go down to the store and sit on the bench out front in the summer, or around the pot-bellied stove in the winter. There were sitting benches out on the courthouse lawn where the old men would come and sit and discuss how the world had gone straight downhill since the good old days. At the garage there were straight backed chairs that you would rock back against the wall, so only the hind legs of the chair were touching the ground. You did not rock chairs back like this at home, because Mama would tan your hide for doing it.

But there among the oil cans and windshield wiper blades, you could kick back and hook your hands over your belly inside your overall bib, and sit.

There are things you can do while you sit. You can whittle little sticks out of big sticks. You can talk. You can shell a pan of butter beans, or watch the cars go by, but your primary purpose is sitting.

Houses used to have sitting rooms, where the grownups would go after Sunday dinner. Mom and Dad and Grandpa and Aunt Rubye would sit and digest the fried chicken and talk about Aunt Ethel's gallstones, and how good the preacher did today. Outside, the children would play, and the afternoon would drift by in a comfortable haze. That sort of thing looks like doing nothing. A recharging battery doesn't look like it's doing anything either. Sitting restores your soul.

We've got more free time now than at any other time since people were invented, and we work so hard at using that time that we don't have a chance to appreciate plain old living. All I'm saying is if you want to enjoy a truly full life, don't just do something, sit there.

# To Be
# Eccentric
# Takes Money
## but
# It Takes Talent
# to Be Weird

# COAT HANGER MENACE

Friends and neighbors, I come before you to sound a warning. We stand to lose the coat hanger as we know it—the wire coat hanger.

One of the world's greatest inventions is the coat hanger—the wire coat hanger. The kind that puts creases across your pants' legs and rust stains on your shirts. Wire coat hangers. The kind that get all bent and gnarled, so when you hang sweaters on them, the sweaters come out gnarled too, and when you wear the sweaters, they make you look like your shoulders grew funny. That kind of wire coat hanger.

Well meaning but misguided individuals have put this noble tool in danger of extinction. They are making coat hangers out of plastic. You don't have to tell me all the advantages of plastic coat hangers. I know they don't rust. I know they keep your pants neater. I know if they start off shaped like a coat hanger, they stay shaped like a coat hanger. Plastic coat hangers work fine...as coat hangers. But they don't work as anything else.

On the other hand, consider the wire coat hanger. A wire coat hanger can rise above its origins. A wire coat hanger may start off as a coat hanger, but it can become, well, almost anything.

When you lock yourself out of your car, what's the first thing you look for? Right. A wire coat hanger. Actually, not many people can open a locked car door with a wire coat hanger but it has several advantages.

The first one is, it gives you something to use to pass the time until the locksmith arrives. It is also a wonderful device for meeting people and making friends. There is something magnetic about a person trying to open his car door with a coat hanger. It attracts all sorts of people. And each of these people want to help.

There may be very few people who actually can open a car door with a wire coat hanger, but there are thousands who believe that they are among those chosen few. I'm not sure if the attraction is the desire to help a fellow human being in trouble, or if it's just the desire to show off.

I would like to tell you all the things you can use a wire coat hanger for—but I can't. There are uses that haven't been invented yet.

Still in the face of this unparalleled utility, we are seeing more and more plastic coat hangers. Just go to the K-Mart and look. They have them in blue and white and red and yellow and pink. All these fat, plastic coat hangers, all shiny and neat and useful-looking, with those notches in the shoulder parts that I think ladies are supposed to hook their dress straps in. All plastic.

Don't misunderstand. I think plastic is fine for toy trucks and credit cards, but I shudder to think of going through life without coat hangers made of wire.

The world is specialized enough. There are plenty of things that do their own jobs and nothing more. A plastic coat hanger is only a coat hanger. It will never be anything but a coat hanger. But a wire coat hanger is raw opportunity. We dare not lose it. If you don't believe me, take plastic coat hangers to your next weenie roast.

# 1,001 USES OF A WIRE COATHANGER
## (USEFUL CONFIGURATIONS OF A FEW BELOW)

ORIGINAL SHAPE

RADIO/TV ANTENNA

ROASTING WEINERS

UNSTOPPING SINKS

HOLDING UP MUFFLERS

UNLOCKING CARS
(BUT ONLY IF IT'S YOUR CAR)

RETRIEVING OBJECTS FROM BEHIND REFRIGERATOR

CAL WARLICK

# CORDLESS TELEPHONE

The only thing wrong with modern conveniences is that old fashioned people have to use them. Take the telephone. There are people among us who remember how, when you wanted to call somebody on the phone, you picked up the receiver and told the operator the number you wanted, and she'd connect you. Then technology took over, and the phone company put a dial on the phone so when you wanted to call somebody, you dialed the number and switches connected you. Now we've got telephones with buttons you mash while the phone plays a little tune and presto! Your phone is ringing the number you called.

Some of us have gone farther than that. We've got cordless telephones with memory features that remember the numbers of everybody we know. This telephone has some wonderful aspects. No longer are you tethered to the wall by a phone cord. You can wander all over the house, jabbering away with your friend, who you have called by pressing the three buttons that summon your friend's number from the telephone's little brain. With a cordless phone, you are freed of wires, freed from taxing your memory with seven digit phone numbers, freed from knowing where your phone is.

Now we can use our memories trying to figure out where it was that we last put down the phone. Back in the bad old days when phones had cords on them, you could start at the wall jack and follow the wire

"RING" RING

until you found, as the phone company puts it, your instrument. You can't do that anymore. Your instrument could be anywhere from the bathroom to the barbecue grill, so every time you want to call somebody, you first have to go on a little treasure hunt, searching for the phone.

Once you have found the phone, you're glad its little brain remembers numbers, because wherever you and the phone discovered each other is usually a long way from a telephone book. You don't need the help of a telephone directory any more. Your telephone can recall all the numbers you need. No longer do you misdial a call and end up with a stranger on the line. Now you press the memory buttons and mistakenly call people you know. If you hit the wrong three keys, you're stuck.

Back when you would dial a wrong number, you could just apologize to the person on the other end, and that would be the end of it. You didn't know who you had called by accident, and the person you called didn't know who you were. It was a nice anonymous mistake. But now when your phone calls somebody you didn't mean to call, it dials the right number...for the wrong person. You know him. And he knows you.

Here you are in a chance encounter, but your wrong friend doesn't know that. He thinks you called him because you wanted to talk to him. And you don't want him to find out that you can't even dial three numbers and get them right. So you tell your friend you called to say hi, and how's your mama, and you hang up feeling like you've gotten through it without making a complete fool of yourself...until you try again, and again you get the same friend.

Nobody calls anybody twice in a row just to say hi. You feel like an idiot. But that's not the worst part. You stumble and stammer and get off the phone the second time, and promptly the telephone dials the same wrong friend again.

It used to be that your friends only suspected you had serious mental problems. Now with the aid of the modern telephone system, they know for sure. Technology and modern conveniences are wonderful. It's great that they make machines smarter. It's just too bad they make people as dumb as ever. It proves nothing is fool-proof.

# Rainy Day Dogs

Have you ever wondered where dogs go when it rains? Well, I'll tell you. Dogs don't go anywhere. Dogs have got some sense. When it's raining cats and dogs, you don't see any dogs, or cats either. The only creatures you see wandering around in a storm are people.

You see people when it rains because they are on their way to their jobs where they work like dogs. But dogs don't work. Especially when it rains. The saying is, "It's lovely weather for ducks." Well, fine, except ducks don't get out in that sort of weather either. Only people. Flocks of people will get out and go sloshing off to work in the middle of a downpour.

The job is there, so you have to be there too, shine or rain. It has something to do with doing your duty and all that sort of thing. I am in favor of duty and responsibility and work, too, as long as I'm not the one who has to do it. But going to work when it rains is unnatural.

When you wake to the sound of raindrops on the roof, what's your first inclination? Right. To roll over and go back to sleep. You want to hole up where it's warm and dry until the rain is over and the clouds go away and the sun comes out, showing the world all washed clean and bright. But what do you do instead? You drag yourself out of bed and get showered and dressed and swill down a gallon or two of coffee and splash out to meet the dreary day with all the other fools on the slippery streets. You know you don't want to be there. Nobody else does either.

What you are doing is flying in the face of nature. Your instincts tell you to stay out of this. You know the natural thing to do is to stay snug and sheltered from the storm, but you can't because you are Man, who has been given dominion over the birds of the air and the beasts of the land. Well explain this to me. If we're supposed to be the boss of all the animals, how come we're the ones who have to go out and work in the rain?

I thought all the other animals were supposed to be there for our benefit, but it looks to me like it's the other way around. Do you know what your dog is doing while you are out there slopping around in the puddles? Your dog has gone in the kitchen and pulled a stool up to the stove, and he has made himself a great big pot of hot chocolate with marshmallows floating in it. And he's gone into the pantry, gotten a loaf of bread, and made a pile of buttered toast. He's put all of it on a tray and taken it into the living room where he has climbed up on your easy chair and is spending the day sitting there eating buttered toast and sipping hot cocoa and watching cartoons and "Lassie" reruns on your TV set. Is that what you are working for, to keep this canine loafer dry, warm, well-fed, and happy? He's not even grateful. If he was, he'd offer to go to the office and fill in for you sometime.

There's a lesson to be learned here. The next time you get to feeling smug about people being the paragon of creation, the highest rung on the ladder of evolution, consider that even a dog is smarter than we are. At least he has enough sense to come in out of the rain.

# ON BANKS

One of the few bad things about Friday is that it's the day a lot of us go to the bank. Now don't misunderstand. I generally like bankers, it's banks...I can't go to the bank without feeling like they don't really want me there. It's the sort of thing that makes a fellow nervous.

There are three ways to go to the bank. You can drive in, you can walk in, or you can go to the automatic money machine. If I've got to go to the bank, I prefer to walk in.

I've tried the drive-in windows, where you sit in the comfort of your car, burning gas and breathing exhaust fumes, while you wait for the person in the car ahead of you to finish collecting the payroll for the United States Army or whatever he's doing up there all that time. When you finally get to the head of the line, you have to hang out your window to get that test-tube looking container out of the thingie that is supposed to take your checks and deposit slip to the teller. Then you put all your stuff in that tube and hang back out to send it through the thingie to the teller.

I worry about where that test-tube is going with my bank business. I figure one of these days the pipe they send it through is going to get a rat stuck in it, and somebody's tube of bank business will be marooned until they can get the rat out. If I use the drive-in window, it will be my tube of bank business. And

then everybody in the bank will come out and claim that it's my rat. I've tried the drive-in. I don't use it anymore.

The same thing goes for the money machines. You've got to stick your bank card in the slot and enter your secret i.d. number before you can do anything. And you know if you make a mistake, there's something inside that machine that's just waiting to jump out and capture your card. That's what the banks call it. Capture. And then you've got to go slinking into the bank and beg them to give you your card back, and you hope they won't ask for ransom to do it. I don't use money machines very much. My nerves can't stand it.

All that's left is to go ahead and walk into the bank and stand in the line. I hate lines. All I want to do is put some money in, or maybe get a little out. But every customer in front of me has a ton of transactions, including asking what happened to the money from the check they deposited ten years ago. Waiting in line behind these folks gives you lots of time to observe your surroundings.

You notice those cameras. You can't glance around without seeing them. But you don't want it to seem like you're looking for cameras because the bank people might think you are casing the joint so you can rob it.

The reason banks have cameras is to make sure bank robbers will have pictures of themselves, but there's no way to know that those same cameras aren't taking pictures of you too. So while you're waiting in line, you have to be careful not to dig or scratch because if the bank ever got mad at you for stopping up the pipe at the drive-in or fouling up the money machine, they could bring out those pictures of you scratching and digging and show them all over town.

There are other things you notice, like the teller to teller-window ratio. Banks want to look big and important and prosperous. That's why they build big buildings with big banking rooms that have ten or twenty teller windows. So how come they only have three tellers? Sometimes they'll have a couple more tellers at the windows, but those will have signs in front of them that say, "Go Away. I'm Busy." I wonder if at any time in recorded history any bank anywhere has ever had all its teller windows open at once.

I think they do all this on purpose to intimidate you and make you feel guilty about coming to visit your money. Oh, they're glad enough to get you to turn your money over to them. Sometimes they'll even give you a toaster or a clock to encourage you to do it. But just try to get a few bucks out, and they'll give you the old fish-eye. They never ask you, but you know they're back there wondering, "Just what does this aspiring felon want this money for?"

So they ask you for all sorts of identification. I didn't ask the bank for identification when I put the money in, so why do I have to provide them with everything from a birth certificate to dental records to get it back out? And that's just to get your own money.

Heaven forbid you should try to get the bank to give you a teensy weensy loan. The only way you can get a bank to let you borrow some of its money is to prove you don't need it.

I have a dream that one day I'll walk into a bank, and it won't have any teller windows or people behind desks. It'll have tables and chairs and flowers and soft music and you'll sit down and the teller will come to you and say, "Hi. I'm Terry. I'll be your teller today. What can I do for you?" And you can give her your order, and while you sit there sipping a Coke or some iced tea, she'll go away and take care of your business. Wouldn't that be nice? If any of you forward-thinking bankers out there want to try this, it's fine with me. I don't charge for ideas. You could send me a toaster, though. Or a calendar. Or an almanac.

# DOUBLE DOORS

A friend of mine named Steve Zumwalt came up the other day with an interesting pair of howcomes. Howcome when a place has double doors, one of the doors is always locked? And howcome you always try to go through the locked one first?

These are the kind of questions that it's amazing to me that nobody has thought to ask until now. Here is a general source of inconvenience and irritation yet, as far as I know, there's never been a major investigation done on the subject.

Well, I've given it a lot of thought, and I believe I've got it figured out. Somebody is out to get us.

You think I'm paranoid? Well, consider the places that have double doors. Banks, Lawyers' Offices, Corporate Offices, your Boss's Office. Now out of that tribe, who wants to nail you? Right! All of them. Behind those double doors, lurk people of power and wealth, and their doors keep you from getting any of either for yourself.

The doors do it by allowing you to make yourself feel stupid. Here you have an entrance designed to look like it is inviting you inside. Most folks don't need two doors. Most of us can fit through one. But here's twice the doorspace, ready to be flung open wide to welcome you...or so one might think.

It's a trap.

Let's say you have finally generated enough courage to go to the boss for a raise. You have practiced what you are going to say, and you've figured out what he is going to say back, and you've come up with the perfect rebuttals to all his arguments. You are ready and primed for action. So you march right up to his office and there, between you and the money you so richly deserve, are two doors. Head up, chin out, back straight, steely resolve in your eye, you reach for the door handle and pull...on the door that's locked. This is not something that you had taken into account in your plans to assault the bastions of management.

You haven't fired your first shot, and already your charge has been repulsed...by the door.

Standing there yanking on the locked side of a double door, your shoulders sag, your jaw slackens, your eyes take on the look of a whipped cur. All your preparations seem worthless. You feel worthless.

How can you think that you're so valuable to the company—that you deserve more money for being there when you don't even have sense enough to go through a door?

You have approached this place with confidence and determination, and now you are a bumbling boob, doomed to failure. It seemed so simple...so easy...two doors beckoning you to come inside. Those doors are there on purpose—to humiliate you. You know as soon as you yank on that door handle and discover you've chosen the wrong one that whoever is on the other side is going to be just as unyielding as that pair of doors. You might as well just slink away and hide.

You are never going to get that raise. You are never going to get that loan at the bank. You are going to go through life pulling on locked doors. The reason that one of a pair of double doors is always locked is to put you in your place. And it works.

That takes care of the first howcome. As for the

reason some of us always choose the locked one...I'm not too sure, but I think the boss has some sort of remote control device inside that can lock whichever side of the door you happen to pull.  I hope that's what it is. I'd hate to think that I was always that dumb.

# Fountain Pen

I saw a story in the newspaper that said the fountain pen is back. Well, I know the newspaper wouldn't lie about a thing like that, so I checked my desk drawer. Sure enough, there was my fountain pen, looking all tanned and well-traveled. I don't know where it went. I don't know how it got out of the desk drawer to go there. The pen didn't say, and neither did the article in the newspaper.

The paper did say that not only is my pen back, but other people are actually buying new fountain pens. And they're paying good money for them. Better than good. People are spending seventy dollars, a hundred dollars, even more...for one fountain pen.

You see, a fountain pen isn't just something to write checks and letters with anymore. It's an accessory. You wear one to complete your ensemble. It is something that makes a fashion statement. It speaks of your lifestyle. Do I need to give you any more hints, or have you already guessed that this fountain pen business is brought to you by the same people who have popularized spinach salads, Brie cheese, mineral water, and expensive German automobiles. You've got it. The yuppies. Young Urban Professionals. The reason they're buying fountain pens is the same as the reason they buy everything else. Status. And ignorance.

You see, yuppies are too young to know anything about fountain pens. They were all raised on ball-points and felt-tips. They don't know that where

67

there are fountain pens, there is ink. There's ink in ball-points and felt-tips, too, but you don't have to deal with it until you start writing. A fountain pen doesn't come equipped with ink. Before you can write with it you have to get the ink out of the bottle...and into the pen. This process will be educational to the Young Urban Professional who elects to try it. He will learn new cusswords. He will learn that not all the ink goes in the pen. A lot of it goes on the yuppie.

Wait until they find out what a blotter is for. Yuppies already have desk blotters. They're a part of designer office sets. I don't believe the yuppies realize those blotters are not just there to cushion their elbows. For that matter, will they actually mess up a desk blotter with nasty old ink, or will they sit there and blow their handwriting dry?

Wait until they learn the joy of having an accessory that dribbles in their pockets. Imagine looking down at a one hundred percent sea island cotton shirt that you paid fifty bucks for and discovering that your three hundred dollar fountain pen has made a fashion statement in blue-black on the breast pocket. Will this remove the pocket protector from the exclusive province of engineers and computer hackers and place it on the bosom of the upwardly mobile?

The fountain pen as status symbol can be fine, as long as you don't use it to write with. There's not much status in reaching for the raw veggies with purple fingers, and not much fun in a lifestyle covered with inkblots.

The yuppies don't know about all this yet, but they will learn. The fountain pen may be an elegant reminder of an opulent yesterday, but sometimes the things from yesterday that we put away in drawers, we put away for a good reason. The pen is mightier than the sword. It is also a whole lot messier.

PANT
PANT

A PAIR OF PANTS   ANOTHER PAIR OF PANTS

## A PAIR OF PANTS

Somebody called a while back with an interesting question. The question is, "Why do we call a pair of pants, a pair of pants?" Normally I don't just throw a question out there if I don't have some kind of an answer, but in this case I don't know the answer. I don't think the man who called had the answer either. I think he passed it along to me for the same reason that I am passing it along to you, because insanity is easier to cope with when you've got somebody to share it with you.

Here is this simple question—why is a pair of pants called a pair of pants. But the more you think about it, the harder the problem is to solve. Since it's driving you crazy, you share it so it will torment somebody else, and you'll have company in your padded cell.

I'll give you the benefit of the thinking that was passed along to me and the thinking that I have added to it. This will give you a head start on going goofy. You don't have to thank me.

The question again, in case you forgot, is, why do we call a pair of pants a pair of pants. A pair of pants is only one thing. A pair of socks is two socks. A pair of shoes is two shoes. But a pair of pants is one...pair of pants. You may think the reason a pair of pants is a pair of pants is because it has two legs. Fine. Now explain why we don't call a shirt a pair of shirts. It's got two arms. And how come a brassiere is just one brassiere. If anything ever deserved to be a pair of...well, let's get back to the pair of pants.

Are you beginning to understand how this can drive you batty? It is the sort of thing that the more you think about it, the more answers you come up with. But the more answers you come up with, the more questions you create. For instance, maybe it's a pair of pants because pants are just the leg part of the pants, like sleeves are the arm part of a shirt. But if that is so, what do you call the part of the pants that isn't the leg part? For that matter, what do you call the part of a shirt that isn't sleeves? See what I mean?

Well, how about the equatorial theory of clothing terminology? Everything you wear from the waist down is a pair. A pair of pants, a pair of socks, a pair of shoes, a pair of undershorts, and everything you wear from the waist up is one. One shirt, one tie, one coat, one hat...one pair of gloves, one pair of glasses, and there goes the equatorial theory right down the drain.

I don't know why a pair of pants is a pair of pants. I have thought and thought about it, and the more I think, the more confused I get. I also don't know who it was that called up and asked me the question in the first place. I wish I did so I could give him proper credit for coming up with it, and we could all go over and burn his house down.

I think the answer to this whole thing may be that there is no answer. A pair of pants is called a pair of pants because it is a pair of pants. This sort of thing is called a paradox. I don't want to think about it anymore.

# Ramp Geeks

When it's summertime, it's boat time. Time to get the old runabout out, crank it up, and zip around the lake, dragging friends and family on water skis. What fun to be afloat, in company with the sun and the wind and the water, and the skiers falling down.

But there are hazards mixed with all this joy. Strange denizens, waiting to prey on the unwary mariner. I do not refer to sea monsters. I refer to a creature of the shore...the ramp geek.

I didn't know that ramp geeks existed until I bought a fifteen foot mini-yacht. The lady at the boat store assured me it was the perfect boat for family outings. She also mentioned that it was a good fishing boat. It was a beautiful craft. The deck was blue with sparkly stuff imbedded in it, the hull gleaming white. There it was, reclining on its trailer, beckoning the family like a siren, tempting us to venture out to sea...or in our case, to lake. Who could resist? Certainly not the Powell family. We loaded the boat with skis and life jackets, and packed the cooler and the picnic basket; we put on our swimsuits, hooked the trailer to the family van, and off we went, typical summer revelers headed for Lake Allanonee. How happy we were in our ignorance. How little we knew. How could we have suspected as we drove lakeward that lurking at the shore, among the picnic tables and trash cans, were ramp geeks?

There is a zone between land and water called the boat ramp. This is the natural habitat and stalking ground of the ramp geek. Of course we didn't know this on our maiden voyage to the lake. All we had on our minds were visions of sunshine and frolic afloat. We gave no thought at all to the part of the trip that calls for getting the boat off the land and onto the water. As we pulled confidently into the parking lot at lakeside, there they were, a half dozen folks lounging on their cars and sitting on picnic tables. They looked like regular people enjoying the day. How could we have known that their entertainment would be us? How could we know they were ramp geeks?

They seemed to be paying us no attention as we pulled the trailer to the launch area. Confident of my ability as a boat captain, I went down the checklist: Drainplug...In. Tiedowns...Unhooked. Winch cable... Unhooked. Life jackets, skis, cooler, lunch basket... Loaded. Any onlooker could see this was a boating family that knew its business.

"Ok, Honey," I called to my wife, "guide me down the ramp."

As I shifted the van's transmission into reverse, I glanced in the side mirror. All I could see was a whole lot of van and a teensy bit of one trailer tire. The bulk of the van hid the rest. From the other side mirror, I couldn't see any trailer at all. It suddenly occurred to me that it's real hard to see a boat trailer behind a van. This discovery led me to the conclusion that the only way I could determine that my trailer was lined up straight behind my truck would be if I couldn't see the trailer at all. I'd be doing it right.

No matter. I had my bride and helpmeet to guide me.

"Come on back," she said, "Go a little to your left."
I turned the wheel a little to the left. The trailer

went to the right.

"No, the other way."

I turned to the right. The trailer went left.

"Not so much."

Suddenly life wasn't as pleasant. And suddenly there were people watching. Drawn to my maneuvers like buzzards to a road-kill possum, a flock of ramp geeks awaited my next move. Leaning on their cars and pickup trucks, perched on picnic tables, their bony necks like stalks held pallid faces turned my way, and beady eyes glowing with a dull light of passionless appreciation.

I pulled the truck forward and got straightened out, then backward I tried again, unsteady as a drunkard. I could see the trailer, first appearing in one mirror, and then the other, as it weaved back and forth until I managed to get the boat and trailer crosswise on the ramp, and the van straddling the curb. I was sweating, and mumbling curses. My bride said, "I think it's stuck." The ramp geeks were silent, but they were enjoying the show. I could tell.

Forward once again, lined up on the ramp, then slowly, unsteadily, I backed down the ramp, carefully ...carefully. The trailer rolled into the water. The boat was afloat. Success! I shifted into Drive and motored forward, pulling the trailer from beneath the boat and up the ramp. Hah!

"A shaky beginning," I thought to myself," But all's well now."

I glanced in the mirror. The boat was serenely drifting away from the launch area, with nobody aboard. The ramp geeks were smiling.

It was at this point that I realized that the ramp geeks were having all the fun. Here I had spent a pile of money for the boat and skis and the rest of it, but was I enjoying myself? No Sir. I was merely an afternoon's amusement for a bunch of people whose only investment was a cooler full of beer and a little gas to drive to the ramp.

It was clear to me that I had been foolish. You don't need a boat to enjoy yourself at the lake. You can have a much better time by becoming a ramp geek. It doesn't cost nearly as much as buying and maintaining a boat, and you don't have to worry about swabbing decks and learning the difference between port and starboard. I recommend it.

Anything in the world is easy as long as you don't have to do it yourself. This is the basis for ramp geekery. The only thing a ramp geek has to do is watch other people. It's the other people who have to do something. They have to back their boat trailers down the ramp and launch their boats.

This may hardly seem the sort of thing that would be a good spectator sport. But those who have never seen it have missed a spectacle. Going forward with a boat trailer is relatively easy. Going backward is something else again...especially when you're not used to doing that sort of thing, and there are a bunch of people watching you.

I am not the only incompetent in the world. There are scores of us, and we're available for entertainment at any boat ramp in this country. You can become a ramp geek by simply going to the lake and sitting around the parking area.

The best time for ramp geeking is a holiday weekend. This is when you have the greatest number of would-be mariners trying to get their boats in the water. It is also a time when experienced boaters stay away, so the ratio of competent boat-trailer-backers to entertaining ones is real low. Just find a comfortable perch with an unobstructed view of the ramp, lean back and enjoy the show.

But there's more for your amusement than just boat-trailer-backing. Remember, the harder time the boater has getting his vessel into the water, the more likely it is that his nerves will be frazzled, thus the more likely that he will do something stupid once he is afloat. You can be sure you'll see the classical Left-the-Drain-Plug-Out, and the Left-the-Boat-Attached-to-the-Trailer routines. There is no end to the madcap zaniness. You'll see unattended boats drift away. You'll see collisions of boat and boat, boat and shore, boat and dock, and boat and trailer. You'll revel in the ritual of Starting-the-Motor-before-It's-Tilted-Down-in-the-Water. Watch in glee as the captain turns red with rage at the Motor-that-Won't-Start. It's all there, and it's all free for the watching.

Late in the afternoon the boaters return, and the fun starts all over again. Watching someone back a trailer with a boat on it down the ramp and into the water is amusing, but the spectacle of backing an empty trailer is even better, and observing as a weary sunburned father tries to manage his temper and a boatload of howling youngsters while getting the boat back on the trailer is the zenith of a ramp geek's pleasure.

Imagine the clowns at the circus. Imagine monkeys at the zoo. Imagine watching a combination of both of them together on the water, and you've got a conservative idea of ramp geeking. There's just one bit of caution I'd like to pass along. The one great unspoken rule of ramp geeking is, do not talk to the boaters. Shouting encouragement and helpful advice is not a good idea. Neither is pointing and laughing hysterically. Boating is supposed to be a restful and soothing sport, but you'd be surprised how testy sailors can get.

# NAPKINS

There are some things in this world that don't make a lot of sense, and the napkin is one of them. It is a prime example of how fashion can ruin civilization. Let's say you are going out to supper tonight. Any place you go, you are going to get a napkin. If you go to a barbecue joint or a catfish place, you'll probably get a paper napkin out of one of those square chrome holders that sit on the table. If you go to a snooty place where the waiter treats you like you don't really have any business being there, you'll probably get a cloth napkin folded up to look like a flower or bird or something else cute.

Whichever kind of napkin you get, where will you put it? Right. In your lap. And what is it for? Right again. To keep you from slopping food on your clothes.

Well that's the part that doesn't make sense. You know as soon as you start eating that a gob of mashed potatoes and gravy is going to jump off your fork and land on your napkin. But it will blaze a trail all the way down the front of your shirt before it gets there. This napkin system may keep your pants looking nice and neat, but your shirt looks like you strained your meal through it.

You don't have to do it that way. You could stuff the napkin in your collar. This is amusing to snooty waiters and your fellow diners because it makes you look like you ought to be eating out of a high chair. This way your shirt will stay clean. But your pants will

get dirty, because whatever you drop will run off the end of the napkin and onto your lap.

Did you ever wonder how we ended up with something that is supposed to keep us neat and tidy but no matter how you use it, it only protects half the territory?

I have been studying this, and I think I've got the answer. Like I said, it's fashion fouling up civilization. The key to the whole thing is in the dictionary. Look up "napkin" in the family Webster's. Right there in the part where it tells you where the word comes from, it says napkin finds its origins in the Latin word, "mappa," which means, "tablecloth."

Now what does this tell us? If the people of ancient Rome said tablecloth when they meant napkin, then it's pretty obvious that back when the Romans were running things, they didn't have little bitty napkins, they had great big tablecloths. When Nero and his buddies sat down for a feast, they'd just scoot their chairs up to the table and grab the bottom of the tablecloth, and stick it in their toga collars. In this way, if you were a guest at one of these functions, you would not have to worry about your party duds getting all messy and you could concentrate on remembering how to speak Latin.

There were other advantages for the dining Romans. If you dropped something that you really liked, like an olive or a hummingbird tongue sandwich, or a deviled egg, it would roll back onto the table where you could get another chance at it. Now wasn't that a neat system? Isn't it logical? Isn't it civilized? Then fashion came along and messed up the whole arrangement, not to mention the togas and trousers of succeeding generations.

One day, Mrs. Caesar decided to have a big dinner party, and she wanted to do something extra, so she thought it would be just the cutest thing to put out a little tablecloth, or "mappakin," next to each guests plate. That way, if the guests dribbled spaghetti sauce on their chins, they could wipe it off with the mappakins and not have to take the big mappa out of their collars. Well, this made sense too, and before you could say "Julius Robinson," every hostess from Gaul to Samaria had heard about the way the Caesars dined and no dinner party or orgy was complete without mappakins for everybody. It got to be the last word in fashion.

This is where the problem came in. Mappakins became so popular that people forgot that they were there to help out the big mappa and started using them to do the whole job. The next thing you know, everybody was getting Roquefort dressing on their ties and barbecue sauce on their pants. And it's gone on like that ever since. For two thousand or so years,

80

we've endured stained clothing because folks were so interested in being stylish they forgot to use good sense.

Now that you know this, you have an option. You can be a slave to fashion and use your napkin, or you can be sane and civilized and do as the Romans did— use the tablecloth. Conform and be messy, or look weird and be clean. But if your mama says use your napkin...use your napkin.

# BEING FAT

A lot of people put on a couple of extra pounds between the holidays. Some folks do it between Thanksgiving and Christmas. A lot more of us do it between
New Year's Day and Christmas.

Ask yourself these questions: Have all your clothes
shrunk? Do you suspect that somebody has been
tampering with your bathroom scales? Do you have to
take the word of others that you still have feet? If you
answered yes to all of the above, some folks may consider you to be chubby.

Does that make you feel bad ? Well consider this.
Maybe fat is the right way to be. It seems to me that
there is good evidence to support this.

For one thing, there are more people who are a tad
overweight than there are who are skinny. If I understand correctly, the way you find out what weight is
average is to put everybody on the scales and add all
those pounds together. Then you count the number of
people there are and divide the total number of pounds
by the total number of people and what you come out
with is the average weight per person, right? So if most
of us are rotund, the average is going to be toward the
hefty side. If to be average is to be normal, and normal is pudgy, that means that skinny people are ab-
normal. They need to start hitting the banana splits
and chocolate cake and macaroni and cheese if they

82

don't want to be out of the mainstream. We normal people will nibble a praline until they catch up.

Now that you see that you are the way you should be, here's more good news. Consider the animals. Animals put on weight to help them through the winter. Bears do it. Beavers and bunnies do it. Whales do it. Since we are members of the animal kingdom, it makes sense that we should store up a little spare blubber too, so a cold snap can't sneak up on us and catch us unprepared.

Fat is warm. Squirrels get fat. Husky dogs get fat. Chihuahua dogs don't get fat. Chihuahuas stand around and shiver a lot. They're no good for pulling a sled either, unless you have a good whip.

In case you are thinking that you should only get fat in winter, remember that most buildings are air conditioned now, so it's really winter to us year round. Have another helping of mashed potatoes and gravy. Have some strawberry shortcake. You don't want to get cold. Being fat is being in tune with nature. Tell them that at the health food store and watch them scream.

Speaking of health, eating is healthy. You have to eat to live, so why not live to eat? It's good for you. It puts a sparkle in your eye and a spring in your step, and gives you an overall feeling of well-being. When a person has a healthy appetite, doesn't that mean that he's healthy? You don't want to wither away from malnutrition, do you?

This goes right back to your childhood. Remember when your mother urged you to eat all the broccoli on your plate because there are so many starving people in the world who would love to have it? Now you've grown up, and out, and there are still hungry people. So you retain the humane obligation to clean your plate. The more zealous of us do it two or three times a meal. It's even easier now that we're big. When you're grown up, you don't have to eat the broccoli if you don't want to. You can fill up your plate with things that you know you'll enjoy while you do your part to wipe out hunger.

Finally, being fat is part of the divine and eternal plan. Most of us get an extra surge of calories during the time around Thanksgiving and Christmas. If God hadn't intended for us to gain weight, how come he put the holidays so close together? And how about all the other religious things? Weddings are religious. What do you do at weddings? You eat cake. How about those chocolate Easter eggs? How about dinner on the grounds? How about church suppers?

I realize that some of you out there don't believe any of this. Some of you may look at all this as a bunch of sorry excuses for not having enough will power to control your appetite. You may be right, but when you're fat, thinking up excuses to stay that way is easier than working to lose those extra pounds. Besides, it helps to take your mind off of how much your clothes hurt.

# SOMETHING TO CHEW BESIDES THE FAT

## *or*

### *Don't Call Me Late for Supper*

# PORK RINDS

It makes you feel important when you can associate yourself with people of power and importance. For instance, I am proud to be able to say, me and the President. I admit that I have never really met George Bush in person, but that doesn't matter in the association game. We do have a couple of things in common, and that's enough. We both like fishing and we both are fond of pork rinds. So now I can say, me and President Bush are going fishing this weekend, and I'll be telling the truth. Of course, President Bush may be going fishing for bonefish or blue marlin in the Florida Keys, and I may be going fishing for bass or bluegills in a five-acre farm pond, but we're fishing together. We're just doing it in different places. Like I said, it makes you feel important.

The same thing goes for pork rinds. As far as I know, Mr. Bush is the first president of the United States of America to admit publicly that he likes to eat pork rinds. Pork rinds, for those of you who have never tried them, are what you end up with when you slaughter the pig and take everything out of the inside of him. Pork rinds are what you've got left. It's the skin. What you do is cut the pig hide into strips and drop them into a great big old pot of hot grease, and they go POING! They puff up like popcorn; that's what pork rinds are, swine popcorn.

Now that you know this, some of you may be swearing off pork rinds for life. If you do it's your loss. They are very tasty, particularly when you sprinkle red pepper sauce on them, which is the way President

Bush and I prefer to eat them.

Pork rinds are great for watching football games. You sit there sunk back in your favorite chair in front of the TV set and watch the football players kick the old pigskin around the field while you gobble up the old pigskin there at home. I don't know if George Bush has an easy chair in front of the TV set at the White House, but anybody who likes fishing and pork rinds should have a good old rump-sprung chair, and I'm willing to bet that the president is no exception.

My only fear is that since we've got a pork rind popping president, they may get to be fashionable. This sort of thing has happened before. Remember how all of a sudden because Ronald Reagan liked jellybeans, everybody started eating jellybeans? Remember how because Jimmy Carter was a peanut farmer, everybody started eating peanuts?

It would be fine if more people eat pork rinds and leave it at that, but once they get fashionable, there are going to be people who want to gild the lily—refine the swine, so to speak. And that means that you'll start finding gourmet pork rinds in a variety of exciting flavors like cheese, and licorice, and blueberry.

I am not making this up. Things like this can happen. They already have barbecue flavor, and that's bad enough. At the store the other day I found pork rinds that are pre-hot sauced. I tried them, and they are worse than barbecue flavor. If they'll try this, sour cream and guacamole flavor is a distinct possibility. I hope and pray that this doesn't happen.

Pork rinds are a simple snack. They deserve to remain simple. The President and I would appreciate it if they leave them that way.

Actually, I don't know if the President will go fishing this weekend or not. But if he doesn't, I'm going without him.

# MOON PIE

Now don't tell me you don't know about the MOON PIE brand marshmallow sandwich.

The MOON PIE is two graham cookies, with marshmallow stuff in the middle, covered with chocolate icing... or sometimes vanilla or banana or peanut butter. There are similar things with different names sold all over the country, but the original is the MOON PIE.

You can find the MOON PIE throughout the Land of Gracious Living, mostly where regular folks want something good to eat that doesn't cost much. It is famous. There has been a book written about the MOON PIE, and at least one song. This has not gone to the MOON PIE's head.

It is a modest product made by a modest company. The Chattanooga Bakery Company has made the MOON PIE since 1917. That one plant in an industrial district in Chattanooga, Tennessee is the world's sole source. You would think they'd have a big sign out front of the bakery saying, "Home of the MOON PIE," but they don't. The Chattanooga Bakery Company doesn't brag. They just keep on cooking up MOON PIE by the millions and sending them out to hungry people from Maryland to Arizona.

The way you say MOON PIE is MOON PIE. That's because that's what it is. It's also because it is a trade name, and the people at the bakery want to make sure that when you ask for a MOON PIE, you don't get something that looks the same but isn't the genuine article. There is something legal about that, but you are supposed to refer to MOON PIE as MOON PIE whether there's one or a million of them.

The way you eat a MOON PIE is, you go in a store and buy one, and buy a Royal Crown Cola. The way you say Royal Crown Cola is RC. It is important that you get an RC Cola, because that is the proper thing to wash the MOON PIE down with. The sweet taste of the RC sets off the sweet taste of the MOON PIE just right. You can ask anybody. But I'm getting off the track. You open your RC and take the wrapper off the MOON PIE and you take a bite of MOON PIE and a swallow of RC, and alternate like that until all of it is gone.

This is a poor man's meal. Lots of folks who work in the mills, or out in the fields depend on it to get them through the day. Back years ago, you could get a MOON PIE for a nickel, and an RC Cola for a nickel. That meant for a dime, you could get something that would keep you going until suppertime. It still works today, but it costs more. For better than seventy years, it's been a southern classic.

## Ode to a MOON PIE

Here's to you, dear MOON PIE
You sure can please a fellow
You're round, you're firm, you're fully packed
With bunches of marshmallow.

With icing made of chocolate, vanilla, or banana
You've made us round as you are,
From Charlotte to Atlanta.

We eat you by the millions here
From Dallas to Montgomery
So thanks for seventy great years
From the bottom of our tummery.

# Boiled Peanuts

A lady wrote me a letter a while back and said, "Why don't you say something about boiled peanuts?"

Well, I thought about it, and thought about it, and I came to the conclusion that when you say some folks like boiled peanuts and some don't, you've just about covered the important points in the boiled peanut department. But then I said to myself, "LeRoy, this lady was not from around here, and she honestly wants to know about boiled peanuts." If somebody comes to

you in search of knowledge, you ought to be honored that he thinks you know something about the subject, and it behooves you to spread enlightenment as best you know how. Besides, there may be other people who don't know about boiled peanuts.

Fall is boiled peanut time. The best place to find them is close to where they're grown. In South Georgia for instance. Here, they take the peanuts straight from the field to the pot while they're still fresh and tender. These are gourmet boiled peanuts. Other places are forced to use the dried article.

If you go driving around in the Fall looking at the leaves in the mountains, you will encounter lots of boiled peanut merchants. They park their pickup trucks right there beside the road. Then they get out a big iron washpot or half of a 55-gallon drum which they set on top of a fire fueled with scrap two-by-four lumber. They pour in some water, dump in a couple handfuls of salt and a bunch of raw peanuts and let her boil. Then they put out a sign that reads, "Boil Pnuts," and wait for business.

There are a couple of subtle things to look for to be certain you are dealing with a genuine boiled peanut merchant who knows what he's doing. The first thing is the sign. If it says, "Boiled Peanuts," be wary. Just about anything else goes, sign and spelling-wise. "Boild" is fine. So is "Penuts." You just want to be careful about signs that suggest excess education.

You also should ask the merchant/peanut chef how much salt he puts in the pot. If he tells you, go someplace else. The amount of salt in the peanut water is about the only variable thing there is in the recipe, and if a peanut cook divulges his secret proportions, he must not have much pride in his product.

But let's say you've found a peanut stand with a properly misspelled sign and a proprietor who looks at you with suspicion and spits some tobacco juice on the ground when you ask about the salt to water ratio, and you buy a sack of peanuts. This is where the important part comes in. You get a peanut out of the shell and try it.

You will immediately notice that there is a difference between the peanuts you are used to and boiled peanuts. Boiled peanuts are wet. They also feel clammy once they cool down a little, but wet is the major sensation. When you crack the peanut shell you discover that the nut inside is just as wet as the nut outside, and you'll find that there is a lot of salty water getting all over your hands, and everything else in the vicinity. The nut itself is not crunchy like a parched peanut. It's firm. And it tastes more like a boiled peanut than anything else.

Some people would rather eat boiled chitterlings than boiled peanuts. Others will take that bag full of stewed goobers and attack it, and not leave anything but a damp sack and a pile of soggy peanut hulls.

Place of birth doesn't seem to have any relationship to whether you like boiled peanuts or not. Neither does economic condition or social status, or age, or race, or religion. If you like your peanuts roasted it's no indication that you'll like them boiled. It's no indication that you won't like them either. The beauty of boiled peanuts is purely in the tastebuds of the beholder.

Some folks like them. Some don't.

# KILLER PANCAKES

Everybody has to have something that he is proud of, something that he can brag about because he has done it or he's good at it or he has discovered it. I am proud of my pancake recipe. Killer Pancakes. I discovered it, I'm good at it, and I do it every chance I get.

The reason I call them Killer Pancakes is not that they will kill you. I call them that because when you eat them, you think you've died and gone to heaven. This sounds like bragging, but it's true. I am good at making pancakes.

The secret is the grits. Grits in pancakes may sound weird, but just hold on until I tell you about it.

Penicillin was discovered by accident. So was vulcanized rubber. So were Killer Pancakes, and they taste better than either of the others.

One morning I was making pancakes for my tiny tots, and halfway through the mixing, I discovered we didn't have enough flour. Being too lazy to start over on something else and too cheap to throw away what I'd already put together, I looked around for a flour substitute. That's when I spotted the instant grits. So I mixed in the instant grits, and eureka! The grits made the pancakes moister, and it gave them an interesting taste and texture that you don't get from your run of the griddle pancake.

Since that morning I've made no other kind of pancake. Once you have found perfection, there's no reason to change. We've given the recipe out over the air at the TV station where I work, and sent recipes by the hundreds, and I'd like to think Killer Pancakes has helped to make mornings happier for a lot of people.

I offer it to you because it's something I'm proud of that I hope you'll enjoy.

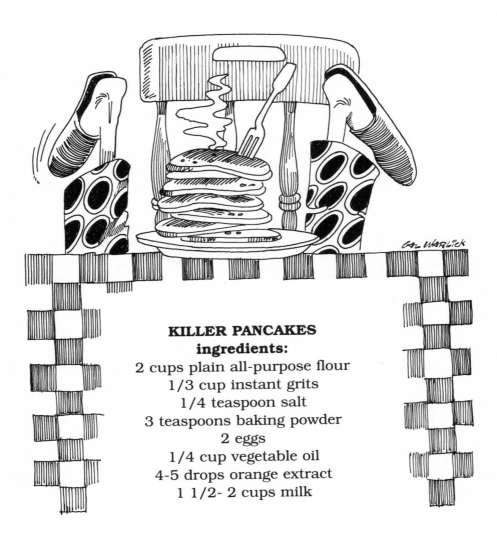

**KILLER PANCAKES**
**ingredients:**
2 cups plain all-purpose flour
1/3 cup instant grits
1/4 teaspoon salt
3 teaspoons baking powder
2 eggs
1/4 cup vegetable oil
4-5 drops orange extract
1 1/2- 2 cups milk

Heat lightly greased electric griddle or skillet to 400 degrees. Mix dry ingredients, then add eggs, oil, orange extract, and enough milk to make it look like pancake batter. Then add a little more milk, because the grits will swell. Pour onto hot griddle, turn when the bubbles on the pancakes break and stay open. Serve with syrup and butter.

That's the basic recipe. You can alter it in several ways. If you want buttermilk pancakes, use buttermilk instead of milk, and add 1/4 teaspoon of baking soda. If you have self-rising flour instead of all-purpose flour, use it, and leave out the baking powder. If you have oranges around the house, you can grate about 1/3 of the rind off an orange and use it instead of orange extract.

There are a couple of other things you should know. Number one is that the recipe calls for instant grits. That means instant grits, not quick grits, not minute grits, not regular grits. If you don't have instant grits, cook whatever kind of grits you have, and add them when you add the liquid stuff. This will cut down on the amount of milk you need. The other thing is that you should use cane syrup for pouring on top of Killer Pancakes. A light flavored honey is O.K. too. Maple syrup or sorghum syrup will overpower the taste of the orange extract.

Oh. One more note. I can't be responsible if your family never wants to go back to regular pancakes again. I warned you they were good before we got started.

# ICED TEA

If you are ever lost and wonder whether or not you are near a big city, all you have to do is go into a cafe and order iced tea. If the waitress asks you whether you want it sweetened or unsweetened, you know you're in town. Away from big towns, which is to say in areas where they know how to do things right, they don't ask this question. They go ahead and serve it sweetened, like it ought to be.

I really don't have all that much against un-sweetened iced tea as long as I don't have to drink it that way. Those who feel like they are a tad on the chubby side and want to cut down so they order un-sweetened tea to go with their mashed potatoes and country fried steak and macaroni and cheese and peach cobbler are welcome to do so.

There are two problems when you order iced tea and it comes unsweetened. The first problem is the shock when you take a big old swig of it and discover there isn't any sugar in there. Once you catch your breath and stop wheezing and coughing, you confront problem number two. How do you get the sugar in? This is simple, but if a restaurant is the kind that will serve you unsweetened iced tea in the first place, chances are they will compound their mistake by making the iced tea harder to sweeten.

When you have to put sugar in your tea yourself, first you get a bunch of those little paper packages that sugar comes in. Then you try to rip them open with-

out spilling most of the sugar on the table, and you pour it in the tea. Then you stir. And stir. And stir. It's hard to get sugar to melt in iced tea. So you have to sit there making your spoon go chingachingaching on the bottom of the glass while you get the tea to where it's worth drinking.

And what do they give you to stir it with? A teaspoon. Teaspoons are for stirring coffee. Iced tea spoons are for stirring iced tea. The handle of a teaspoon is too short. You have to grasp the handle by a fraction of an inch of the very end to get it down far enough in the iced tea glass to reach to where the unmelted sugar is. And no matter how hard you try to avoid it, you keep baptizing your fingers in your tea.

If restaurants want to serve, they ought to learn to serve right. Especially tea. And I haven't said anything at all yet about the lemon.

It's a shame. I know iced tea is a strange drink. You boil it to make it hot, and put ice in it to make it cold. Then you put sugar in it to make it sweet, and lemon in it to make it sour. I realize this is peculiar, but it works, and I don't think we need to mess with it. Except in the lemon department. I am referring, of course, to the growing practice of serving lemon slices with iced tea.

You know how they do it. Somebody back in the kitchen slices the lemon from side to side, so you have these round disks of lemon—half a disk if they want to be cheap about it. The waitress brings you a big fat glass of iced tea, and there's this skinny lemon slice hanging on the side of it. Now that may look stylish, but it doesn't work. You are supposed to have the lemon there so you can squeeze it into your tea. Have you ever tried to squeeze a lemon slice? Lemon slices are too thin. You can't mash them, you have to mangle them. And that is messy. You get as much lemon juice on you as you get in your tea glass.

The way to fix a lemon for iced tea is to cut it in wedges, from the top of the lemon down. A lemon wedge is useful. You can mash it and get some juice out of it. And you can get the juice where you want it, not in your eye or on your shirt. It seems to me that the folks in the kitchen would find that it is no harder to cut a lemon from north to south to produce wedges than it is to cut it from east to west and end up with useless slices.

I don't have any grand ambitions in life. I would just like to perform some small service for my fellow man, so that when I go, people will feel that their world is a little better because I have been there. If I could get restaurants to learn how to serve iced tea right, I could die satisfied that I have done my part. A sprig of mint would be nice too, but that may be asking too much.

# RED PEPPER SAUCE

There are two things in this world that we will never run out of, because no matter how hard you try, you can never use it all up. Those two things are mother's love and red pepper sauce. You already know about mother's love, but red pepper sauce ranks right up there with it in the inexhaustible supply department. I am referring to red pepper sauce, not white pepper sauce. Red wines and white wines go with different foods, and so do red and white pepper sauces.

White pepper sauce goes with turnip greens and collards and boiled cabbage. You get your greens on the plate and give them a real healthy dose of white pepper sauce. That is the sauce that comes in a bottle that is full of little green hot peppers.

There are no little green peppers in the red pepper sauce bottle. There are no peppers of any color in there. There's no way to get them in there. I don't even know how they get the pepper sauce in there. The bottle is all glass, with one little bitty hole in the top. I know it must be hard to fill the bottle, because getting the sauce out is a bear. You can only get a little drop at a time.

That's the way it should be, since a little dab will do the trick on your eggs, or oysters, or black-eyed peas, or pig ear sandwich, or any of the zillion other things that red pepper sauce improves.

You can run out of white pepper sauce—especially if you like to dig in the bottle and get a pepper or two out and cut them up in your greens—but despite all the things you use red pepper sauce for, you always have some sauce left in the bottle. It stays with you. And it doesn't go bad. You can keep a bottle of red pepper sauce for years and years and the next time you use it, it'll be just as spicy as it was the last time. People have tried it, and it's true.

When you finally do get down to the bottom of the bottle, you're still not out. There's a drop or two that gets down there in the corner and hangs on, and no matter how hard you try, you can never get it out. You've got it forever.

Mother's love is the same. No matter what you do, no matter how many times you slight her, and neglect her, and forget to send her a Mother's Day card. No matter how rotten you get and how low-down and worthless you are in the eyes of the rest of the world, you've still got your mama. Her supply may get awfully low, but way down in the corners of her soul, she's always got just a little bit of love left for you. You already know that, but I figured you would like to know that the red pepper situation is in good shape too. And besides, red pepper sauce goes better with oysters.

# CULTURAL
# TIDBITS

# GNAT SHOOING

If you come from certain parts of the country, there are things that you are born knowing how to do. Folks from below the Macon-Dixon Line have an innate knowledge of gnat shooing. Even eensy weensy children can do it. Since everybody you know knows how to shoo gnats, you assume that everybody everywhere knows how. You don't think of it as a unique regional skill until somebody from somewhere else shows up.

People from somewhere else are not born knowing gnat lore. That is why it's so easy to tell who's a tourist in, say, Camilla, Georgia. Tourists in south Georgia in the summertime look real friendly, like they are waving at everybody all of the time. What they are trying to do is shoo the gnats away.

Gnats, if you are not familiar with them, are little bitty bugs that fly around your eyes and nose and ears and generally try to get familiar with you. Gnat country is that whole section of the Land of Gracious Living known as "Below the Gnat Line." Here, the landscape flattens out into coastal plain, the pine trees grow tall, and the gnats grow numerous. Gnats sit around all day doing nothing until a person shows up. Then they take off like a great insect air force, a gnat armada, a cloud of amiable bugs, who only want to fly into your ears or up your nose or into your eyes. Many people find this disturbing.

This is where gnat shooing comes in. You want to get the gnats away from you, but you want to do it with the effortless style and grace of a native. Waving your hands in front of your face to shoo gnats will only wear you out and mark you as a stranger.

You want to shoo the gnats without using your hands. It's simple. Every barefoot kid in the region knows how to do it. First you casually inhale through your nose—casually, so as not to excite suspicion among the gnats that you're up to something. Then you stick your lower lip out, off to the left side of your face. This forms a passageway which, when you puff slightly, sends a column of air up towards your left eye. This blows the gnats away from that side of your face. Then you repeat the procedure on the right side of your face to de-gnat it too.

This method is more difficult to describe than it is to do. Practiced gnat shooers can do the no-hands-gnat-shoo while carrying on a conversation and not miss a syllable. It's just a quick puff left, puff right process, but it works. You don't have to thank me. I am glad to share this sort of cultural tidbit in the interest of inter-regional understanding.

Incidentally, if you have a moustache, the no-hands-gnat-shoo doesn't work very well. What happens is, your moustache gets in the way of the flow of air and diverts it away from your eyes. You end up shooing the gnats away from your ears, instead. If you have ever wondered why moustaches are not very popular along the southern coastal plain, that is the reason.

Incidentally, you may also wonder why somebody would want to learn how to shoo gnats away without using his hands. That's simple. It's so you can hold an RC Cola in one hand and a Moon Pie in the other.

# CELTS

It has become popular these days to dig around in archives and find out who all your ancestors are. When you do that, you get to brag about where you came from and who you are related to. I am not the kind of person who takes on a job like that, but some of my relatives are. When they came back with their report, there was good news and bad news.

The bad news is we Powells don't seem to have very many pirates, cattle rustlers, and desperadoes in our past. This may explain why we Powells don't have a great deal of money.

The good news is that the Powell family originated in Wales, in what is now southwest England. The Welsh are an ancient people, who are known as dreamers, adventurers, and poets. Brendan Behan was Welsh. So was Richard Burton. So was Saint Patrick. Saint Patrick was a Welsh monk who did more than run the snakes out of Ireland. He also brought uisquebaugh in. More on the uisquebaugh business later.

The Welsh are descendants of the Celts. That is more good news. Anybody with Celts in their background can take pride. If you enjoy gracious living, thank a Celt. The Celts were barbarians who used to run around central and western Europe before all the other bunches of barbarians came in and ruined the place. That's the way it is. You find a perfect spot, and the next thing you know, every Angle, Saxon, Pict, and Jute in the world wants to go there and crowd you out.

108

The Celts knew how to enjoy life. That was their downfall. Work was not a popular word in their vocabulary. The Celt national motto was, "If it ain't broke, don't fix it. If it is broke, don't fix it either. Go out and steal another one."

The flowering of Celtic culture (I know it's an oxymoron) occurred between 1200 and 400 BC. For 800 years, the Celts were the political and cultural (here we go again) leaders of their neighborhood. In 800 years the Celts managed to come up with three inventions. This may not seem like much inventing for 800 years, but they probably weren't trying the whole time.

Two of the Celtic discoveries were wicker and liquor. I think wicker came first. The reason I think this is I have seen wicker furniture, and it looks like it takes a certain amount of concentration to weave together into something that you can recognize, much less trust enough to sit down on. You already know the Celts were bad to be worthless. If they had liquor before they had wicker, it doesn't take a genius to figure out that instead of inventing wicker, they would have invented a pile of sticks.

So there the Celts were, weaving away on their porch furniture, and then they invented liquor. They called it "uisquebaugh," which means "water of life." You can tell they were awfully proud of it. They were also their own best customers. This shows you how fortunate the Celts were to already have the invention of wicker under their belts before they got uisquebaugh under there too. It gave them a comfortable place to sit once standing became worrisome.

The invention of uisquebaugh could have been the last notable thing the Celts did if it hadn't been for their basic playful spirit. The whole Celt tribe would sit around in their wicker chairs, soaking up uisquebaugh and thinking of merriment. And if a stranger should

109

happen by, the Celts would invite him to enjoy the festivities with them.

First, they'd fill his tank with uisquebaugh. Then when he was in a receptive state of mind the head Celt would invite him to rest in a great big wicker basket. Once the guest was all comfortable in his basket, the Celts would gather around it, singing songs and dancing. Then the head Celt would light a ceremonial fire under the basket. Imagine how surprised the unwary guest was! What good fun! The Celts could hardly wait until another stranger showed up so they could start all over again.

The problem with doing this sort of thing is after a while you start to run short of unwary guests. For weeks at a time the Celts would sit there by the side of the road hoping to see an unfamiliar face, but nobody came. This was beginning to erode the famous Celtic cheerfulness. Some of the tribe began to entertain themselves by playfully whacking their neighbors over the head with large sticks. The neighbors, getting into the spirit of the frolic, would hurl stones at their attackers. The head Celt, seeing that this sort of sport could cut way down on the available number of voters in the next election, decided that something had to be done.

Since the games of Incinerate the Tourist had proved so popular, the head Celt figured a way to amuse his constituents without having to depend on stray travelers.

It was a brilliant solution. He simply issued a decree declaring each pig in the tribe's swine herd an honorary stranger. Celt life became a lot happier right away. Now the tribe could have a frolic whenever they wanted without having to lie in wait for somebody to put in the basket. They would simply select an honorary stranger from the pigsty, put him in the basket,

110

and light it up.

Eventually this pastime developed and evolved into the pinnacle of Celtic achievement. Since it seemed like a lot of trouble to make a basket for a pig, and since the pigs were honorary strangers anyhow, only symbolic representations of something else, the tribe would gather a pile of hickory limbs and declare it an honorary basket. The tribe also found that if you kept the pig over the bed of hot hickory coals for several hours, he was real good to eat, especially if you anointed him with a spicy sauce.

Honored tribe members became masters of the ritual, presiding over the glowing coals, commanding their assistants when to turn the pig, and guarding the secret of the sauce.

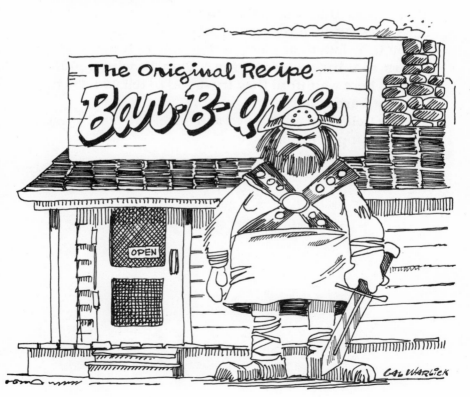

Throughout the uncivilized world rumor quickly spread of this new and wonderful method of transforming a pig into something near heaven. Surrounding tribes hurried to Celt country to try this new invention and brought their appetites with them. There were so many new people showing up for the swine rituals that the Celts hardly had a bite left over for themselves. All this crowding forced the Celts to retreat to remote corners of the British Isles, which they named Scotland and Wales and Ireland. There the Celts continued to make uisquebaugh and sing songs and write poetry. They do it even today. You may wonder about the pig ritual. Well, it was exported to the New World with the early settlers and is practiced still where Celt descendants and their friends appreciate the finer things of living. In this country we call it barbecue, and we remember how a slothful but fun loving tribe lost their place at the table to hungry outsiders seeking a good thing. That is why people around here wait until they trust you to tell you where the best barbecue is.

We Celts already got overrun once. We don't want to let it happen again.

# COON HUNT

Hunting coons is a lot like eating chitterlings. If you do either of them once, you never have to do it again. It's like being vaccinated. One unpleasant dose will protect you. After one serving of chitterlings, for instance, you have an excuse that will keep you chitterling-free forever. From then on, if anybody asks you if you want some chitterlings, you can say, "No thank you, I had some already." I had my chitterlings ten years ago. I don't want any more. Coon hunting is like that too.

The raccoon is a very intelligent animal. I wish I could say the same for coon hunters. Some people around here get great pleasure out of coon hunts and go every chance they get. I figured it must hold some attraction that you can't see from a distance, so one January evening, I hooked up with a bunch of boys in Newton County, Georgia for a night of adventure.

The way you go coon hunting is you get together with a crowd of other coon-seekers and their coon dogs and head for the woods in the middle of the night. When you get to the woods, you turn the dogs loose. Then you wait—a cluster of full-grown men wearing hip boots and hard hats with little headlights stuck to them—and listen to the dogs bark. I don't have to go to the middle of the woods to hear dogs bark. I have a dog at my house.

But coon hunters love this. They know each dog's voice. Each hunter knows what his dog is saying to him. They do not speak Dog, but they understand it fluently.

You are standing around in the woods, a pack of dogs is running around howling in the dark, and the coon hunters are having a grand old time. You, the initiate, are just freezing to death. Weather is very important in coon hunting. It has to be cold enough to be really uncomfortable or the hunters are not happy. Somewhere out in the darkness is a coon, and he is likely, when pursued by a pack of dogs, to climb a tree. The dogs report to their owners on the progress of the chase.

"ARROOOO"

"That's Blue." (All coon dogs are named Blue, or Ranger, or Rattler. None of them are named Fifi or Spot.)

"ARROOOO"

"She's struck!"(That means somebody smells a coon)

"ARROOOO"

"They're going through the swamp."(Remember this swamp. We'll come back to it later.)

"ARROOOO"

"She's treed!"

Oh boy! When the dogs tell their owners that they have a coon up a tree, you get to spring into action. You get to go down in the swamp. (Remember the swamp?)

One of the rules of coon hunting is that there must be a swamp involved. That is why coon hunters wear those hightopped rubber boots. The other rule of coon hunting is that the water in the swamp has to be two inches higher than the top of those boots. (The swamp rule can be waived when you go coon hunting in the mountains, provided there are cliffs available to fall off of.)

So you plunge into the swamp in pursuit of the dogs, with the limbs whacking you in the face and the icy water pouring into your boots. The only light you have is either a carbide lantern or an electric light

hooked on the hard hat that you wear because a regular hat would be too comfortable. There is enough light to see the thing that you are about to run into after it's too late to get out of the way.

I used to think that you went coon hunting at night for the benefit of the coon. You don't. You go coon hunting at night because if you could see where you were going, you wouldn't go there.

Picture yourself fighting your way through the briars and the brambles. You're stuck and scratched and bruised and bleeding. Finally you make your way to that island in the swamp. And there stands a tree with a bunch of dogs hollering up it, indicating that this tree, in the opinion of the dogs, is the tree that contains the coon.

It is at that point, in the middle of the swamp in the middle of the night, that you find out that coon dogs will lie to you. There is not a coon up that tree. There hasn't been a coon up that tree. There is not going to be a coon up that tree.

I think coons enjoy coon hunting because it gives them a chance to make fools out of a bunch of dogs and people. The hunters and their dogs seem to enjoy it too. Like I said, you can't testify to the intelligence of coon hunters.

You may think this is the end of the story. It's only the start. The dogs hollering up that tree are not all the dogs that you turned loose earlier in the evening. The majority of the pack is three or four miles away, begging scraps at the back door of a Waffle House out on the four-lane. You spend the remaining hours of the night trying to round up the rest of the coon hounds. They really ought to call it "dog hunting," but I guess the animal lovers might misunderstand and get all over them if they did.

# Snow Driving

If you are not from The Land of Gracious Living there may be a couple of things you were not raised on. Eating grits is one that leaps immediately to mind. You also may not be familiar with how to put peanuts in a bottle of Coca-Cola or how to say things like, "Howsyomamanem."

Those of us from around here grew up on that sort of thing, and we are glad to share these cultural tidbits with newcomers. We are glad to have people from other parts of the country dwelling among us. It shows that even though they have the misfortune to be born someplace else, they can still rise above their origins and come to live here.

These people who are from someplace else have things they were raised up on too, like knishes and stickball and knowing how to drive in the snow, and these folks seem to think that we need to know such things, especially the part about driving in the snow.

It snows around here once or twice a year, and every time it does, all the people who are not from around here feel like they have to tell us how it snows a whole lot more where they're from, and how we don't know how to drive in the snow that we do have. Well, they're right. It only takes an inch of snow to shut Dixie down. When it snows around here, the schools all close, and people are afraid to get out of their driveways. Those who do venture out are even worse. We have folks running off the roads and slipping and slid-

117

ing and crashing into each other and getting stuck at the bottom of hills. And the traffic just stops.

This has to look strange to people from Minnesota, for instance, or Vermont, or Colorado. When it snows in those places, it snows feet, not inches. In these places, there's snow on the ground most of the winter, and the people who live there go about their business like nothing unusual was happening. And then they move South, where a mere dusting of snow paralyses the entire area.

I can understand their urge to tell us ignorant natives that we're incompetents on an icy road. But we ignorant natives don't want to hear it. What we have here is a cultural misunderstanding. Well-meaning foreigners think that we will appreciate their superior skills and knowledge in the ice and the slush, and that if we will only listen to them, then we can learn to get around as easily as they do. These people mean well, but they are misguided.

We don't want to learn to drive in the snow. Now think about this. How often does it snow in the North? All the time. How often does it snow in the South? Maybe two times a year, and then it's only on the ground a day or two. Since it doesn't snow all the time around here, why should we want to learn to cope with it?

The way things are now, every time it snows we get a holiday. Nobody goes to work or school, and we all go outside and take pictures and make snowmen and slide down hills on whatever we can turn into a sled for a day. Some of us find somebody we love and go for a walk, or just sit inside and look out the window and think about how pretty it all is. Then the next day when the snow has melted, we go back to work and school and get on with the regular routine. Now tell me why should we give up a couple of unscheduled

118

midwinter holidays by learning how to navigate an icy street? Why should we exchange a day of fun and magic for just another day on the job?

When it comes to driving in the snow in the South, we're ignorant and want to keep it that way. In this case, y'all, ignorance is bliss.

# PEACHTREE STREET

It just takes a little thing, a mere accident of fate, to determine the entire course of the future. Now you take for instance the story that Atlanta owes her position as a premier city of the Land of Gracious Living to baseball loving Indians from South Carolina. You see, way back when the Indians were running things, there was a tribe in South Carolina that was really crazy

about baseball. Every year they would load up the squaws and papooses and come down to Atlanta to take in a Braves game or two.

Now Atlanta was not the same then as it is today. There weren't hamburger joints on every corner up and down the road. There was no Varsity where you could get an order of chili dogs and good old greasy onion rings. Back then, you wanted something to eat, you either had to bring it with you, or hunt it down once you got here. And when you're going to a ball game, you don't want to stand a chance of being late because you're out stalking a buffalo or trying to call a turkey into easy arrow range. So these folks from South Carolina packed their lunches.

One thing they always did was bring a sack full of peaches. They grow a bunch of peaches in South Carolina. Before the ball game in Atlanta, the Indians would have a tailgate party with deviled eggs and roast deer and all those peaches. And they would throw the peach seeds on the ground because there weren't any trash cans.

Well, there was a creek near where they had these picnics. And the peach seeds washed down the creek, sprouted alongside it, and grew into peach trees. There were so many of them that they started calling it Peachtree Creek. At the mouth of the creek was a town, and the people living there called the town Standing Peachtree. And they named the trail leading to their town Peachtree Trail. That's how the most famous street in Atlanta got its name. I heard this story from a man standing in the line behind me at the tax office the other day. He said he got it from an old Confederate veteran who must have gotten it from an old Indian. I have no idea if it's true or not, but I think it's as good a story as anybody else has come up with.

At any rate, today there are more Peachtree

Streets in Atlanta than you can shake a switch at. I looked at the map, and there are 28 different streets named Peachtree something. That's because everybody in Atlanta wants to have a Peachtree address. Do you remember what I said about the future of a city being determined by accidents of fate? It's just by chance that they named Peachtree Street after the town on the creek with all the peach trees on it. They could just as easily have named it for what was on the other end of the road—Hog Mountain.

Now I am as big a hog fan as anybody, but Hog just doesn't have the same panache that Peachtree does, namewise. Do you think Atlanta would be what it is today if the main road was Hog Street? Would there be Hog Terrace and Hog Park Place and Hog Circle and all the other Hogs that are Peachtrees now? No. Would tourists want to stay at a hotel called the Hog Plaza? Would businesses want to have their offices in Hog Center? Would the people publishing this book call themselves Hog Publishers? Not likely.

If the most fashionable address in town conjures up visions of swine, there's no chamber of commerce on earth that could promote it. So nobody would have moved to Atlanta, and the town would still be a little crossroads that never amounted to anything. Atlanta can be thankful to the Indians and their sloppy eating habits, and to the providential circumstance that chose Peachtree over Hog.

You may wonder why there aren't still a bunch of peach trees around here. Well, peach trees get old and die. And the Indians with the peaches haven't come back lately, because the Braves haven't been worth watching.

# JULY 5TH

Have you ever noticed how fearless and strong all the good guys of history are? Take our own Founding Fathers, Tom Jefferson, Ben Franklin, all that bunch. Remember how on July 4, 1776, they all marched bravely up and signed the Declaration of Independence. John Hancock even signed great big, with a flourish, so it would be easy for King George to read. We can be proud of what they did, determined men staking their future on the righteousness of their cause. They were fearless, they were strong—on the fourth of July. I just wonder if they still felt the same way on July 5th.

Just imagine if you were John Hancock, waking up the next morning and realizing that you're in deep, deep trouble. Not only have you signed a document telling your monarch to put his empire where the sun never rises, you have signed it bigger than anybody else. There it is, a nice, legible signature, your own John Hancock. You know that your name is the first one the king will see, and if he can't take a joke, you're the first one he's going to come looking for. You couldn't have a nice illegible squiggle of a signature, no, not you, not big John.

It was probably the same with all the guys. Yesterday, it seemed like a real good idea. You get a bunch of fellows from all over the country together at a convention, and everybody gets to talking big about "no taxation without representation." Those guys from Boston bragging about dumping the tea in the harbor. Tom Jefferson and Ben Franklin whooping it up and cheering everybody on. Heck, yeah you signed. Who wouldn't? Throwing the British out seemed like a dandy notion...at the time.

But it's the next day when you get to thinking about it, and you tell your wife, who says, "You signed a declaration of WHAT?"

You might just begin to wonder if just maybe you have made the wrong move.

There are very few of us who have personally ever signed a declaration of independence, but most of us have signed a few documents like house notes and car notes and contracts for dancing lessons. You always wake up the next day wondering if you did the right thing then, and all you've signed away is your money. When the founding fathers put quill and ink to parchment, they signed away their fortunes too, not to mention their lives and sacred honor. Saying you're going to kick the British out is one thing, signing a paper that pledges you to kick the British out is something else again, especially when you realize that the British army is already there, and they carry guns.

I don't know if that's the way it happened, but if they were like the rest of us, it is. You take the case of

Button Gwinnett. He was there as a delegate from Georgia. A Button Gwinnett autograph is one of the rarest signatures there is. After he signed the Declaration of Independence, you couldn't hardly get him to sign anything anymore.

We can be glad that things turned out fine for the patriots. They backed their words up with action and won freedom and founded a great nation based on the ideals they set forth and endorsed on July 4, 1776. We can never know if they could imagine that two hundred and something years later, we'd be honoring them with fireworks and barbecues and baseball games. But I'm willing to bet that on July 5th, they gave the future a whole lot of thought. A fellow just can't be too careful about what he signs.

# Eagles, Turkeys, and Ducks

Let me start off by saying I have nothing against eagles. I have nothing against turkeys, either. But do you realize that when it came time for the guys who started this country to pick a national bird, the only fowls placed in nomination were the turkey and the eagle? It's true. That was back in 1782. We had just fought and won our independence by beating the British, so now was the time for forming our own government—not to mention naming our national bird.

This is not a mystery story. You already know what happened when the votes were counted. You know the eagle won. And you know this didn't please Benjamin Franklin even a little bit because he was the leading spokesman for the turkey faction. Franklin figured the eagle was a symbol of a lot of empires, which is something he didn't want this country to have. He liked the turkey because it's from around here and it ought to have the hometown vote. Benjamin Franklin was a great man, and a great thinker, but when it came to national birds, the turkey wasn't one of his better ideas.

Just think of the turkey, symbolwise. Our national symbol should reflect the way the people in the country feel about themselves. Do we think of ourselves as turkeys? I think not. Do you think America would have grown to the great nation it has become if we had a turkey sitting on the top of the flagpole at the courthouse, or standing there on the Great Seal,

clutching a bunch of arrows in one hand and a bunch
of olive branches in the other? It's just hard to believe
that other countries would be able to take us seriously.
How hard would a boy work to become a Turkey
Scout?

On the other hand, how would you like to square dance to a tune like Eagle in the Straw? The turkey is a whole lot better off where it is, belly up on a platter at Thanksgiving. But I think that brother Franklin had a point when he objected to the eagle. Everybody has eagles. The Romans had eagles, the Germans have eagles, the Mexicans have eagles, the Austrians even have an eagle with two heads.

Ben Franklin was right to want something more original in the national bird department. It's just a shame he didn't think past the turkey. He might have had a better chance if he had proposed the duck.

Now there is a noble candidate for national bird. The duck. It's a lot like Benjamin Franklin. Versatile, enthusiastic, outgoing, clever. It's a symbol the nation could be proud of. Ducks are smarter than either turkeys or eagles. Ducks not only can fly, they can swim, too. Let's see an eagle or a turkey do that.

When storm clouds gather, it doesn't bother the duck. The rain just rolls off his back. Ducks appear proud and serene on the surface, but underneath, they're paddling like crazy. And here's the best part. Ducks are peaceful. Ducks don't bother anybody. And everybody likes ducks. Aren't all these duckly qualities things that our country would like to be known for?

I realize that in 1782, the founding fathers had a lot of important things to do like putting tax on whiskey and writing a constitution, but I think it's a shame they had such a limited slate of candidates when it came time to pick the national bird.

When you've got a duck, you never miss the boat. When you've got a duck, you don't need a boat. We even had a president named for a duck. Mallard Fillmore.

# THE MAN WHO WILL BE KING

I think some people in America resent the fact that when we won the Revolutionary War, we kicked the royalty out along with the British. They think it's unfair that they can't be the Baron of Valdosta or the Earl of Talladega or the Duchess of Social Circle. We do have the Dukes of Hazzard, but that's something altogether different.

Nobility is a dandy idea as long as you're one of the nobles. The problem is that everybody wants to be royalty and nobody wants to be a loyal subject. Look around your neighborhood. How many of the folks on your block do you want to call "Your Grace" or "Your Highness"? Well you can bet that they feel the same way about you.

Kings are fine for countries who want them, but it suits me right down to the ground that our only nobles are in the Shrine Club. Besides, it's not that easy being king.

Prince Charles over in England will be King Charles one of these days. It sounds like a good job, but just think about it. First of all, kings have to be pleasant all the time, and they can't sweat. Worst of all, you can't get the job until your mother dies. I couldn't live like that.

You might think it's easy, once you get your attitude adjusted and your sweat glands tied off. Just sit around on the throne all day and whack folks with a sword to turn them into knights. But being royalty cuts way down on your career options.

Charles will be King of England someday. There's no question about that. He doesn't have much to say about the matter. Neither do any of the rest of the royal family. They're royalty, and there's nothing they can do about it. Prince Andrew flies a helicopter for the RAF, but nobody thinks of him as a helicopter pilot. He's a prince. He always will be a prince, unless he does something nasty like take Charles for a helicopter ride and dump him out over the English Channel. That way, Andrew can advance to king. But it's not thought of as a nice thing to do, even among royalty.

Andrew and Charles were born princes and they have to do prince stuff. If Charles wanted to run a fishbait store or sell insurance policies or be a fireman, he couldn't. He's got his future already lined up. He was born to be king. That's all he can be, even if he is not good king material. There's only one Prince of Wales, and he's it.

It's different in this country. Nobody is born into a job here. In America, you have the whole range of vocational possibilities open to you, from architect to zoologist. The circumstance of your birth doesn't force you into anything. If you want to break your mother's heart and stoop to the pursuit of politics, all you have to do is fool enough people long enough to get yourself elected, and there you are. On the other hand, if you have loftier ideals and your interest and aptitude takes you into the waste management field, you are absolutely free to become a garbageman.

We are fond of saying that in America any kid can grow up to be president, but there's something a lot more important. In America, no kid is required to.

130

# CHICKEN FAT AND HAIR

I guess that when you're a researcher, finding out about stuff is your goal in life, and you don't really care to figure out what your discoveries are good for. You leave the practical applications to other people. Take chicken studies, for instance. The poultry industry is real interested in how to make chickens grow faster and grow bigger, and that means there's all sorts of chicken research going on all the time. I don't have any argument with that. It's just that the scope of this research needs to be expanded. Things they are discovering about chickens might very well apply to people, too.

A very fine example of this is the study that showed if you play classical music to chickens, the chickens gain weight faster.

An animal psychologist did the research. He hooked up a stereo system in the hen house and piped music in amongst the pullets. He found that you get a two to three percent chubbier chicken when the coop is tuned in to the works of Antonio Vivaldi. The hens would rather listen to Vivaldi than Willie Nelson or Elvis or anybody.

This is the sort of scientific finding that appeals to two kinds of people, chicken growers, and classical music fans. The chicken growers see bigger chickens as that much more chicken meat they can put on the shelves at the Kroger store, and that much more money they can put in the bank. Classical music fans

131

see results like these as another reason to feel smug and superior.

Researchers have pulled this same music appreciation stunt with cows and houseplants too—with the same results. The more classics you play, the more growth you get.

Now I am all for chicken growers making a few more buck buck bucks, and I don't have anything at all against the crowing by classical music fans, but I'm afraid nobody is pointing out the real discovery here. Think about it. Chickens grow better with Vivaldi. So do cattle. So do petunias. Doesn't this tell you something? Of course it does. It tells you that classical music will make you fat.

It's as plain as can be. Look at the research. More than that, look at the people connected with classical music. What do Luciano Pavarotti, Itsak Perlman, Leontyne Price, and Joan Sutherland have in common beside being in the Mozart game? Right. They are stylish stouts, each and every one.

It comes from all that rich Bach and Beethoven and Verdi and Vivaldi. Now don't go pulling out a bunch of ballet dancers on me. I know Nureyev and Barishnikov are skinny, but they get enough exercise to work off all the calories Tschaikovsky throws at them. Your regular classical music person just sits there and soaks up all those high calorie symphonies and sonatas, and puts on the lard. Tonight it's music to your ear, tomorrow it's fat upon your rear. If you love Handel, you'll develop love handles.

Now that you know about this, you can use it for something better than raising fat chickens. Tell your wife that it's a scientifically proven fact that classical music makes you gain weight. You may never get dragged to another opera.

Now do you see what I mean about doing research

without worrying about what it's good for? This sort of thing is wasted on chickens, but for you and me it's got real practical applications.

The same thing goes for the seawater and feathers research. This one was done at the University of Georgia. A research associate at the Poultry Disease Research Center discovered that if you add ten percent seawater to a chicken's water dish, it makes the chicken's feathers grow stronger.

Now why, you may ask, would you want to make a chicken's feathers stronger? It's because when you get a couple hundred thousand chickens in a chicken-house, they tend to rub together a lot, and that wears their feathers off. And a featherless chicken spends more time shivering than it does growing big drumsticks or laying eggs. So you feed them seawater, and it makes their feathers stronger and harder to rub off.

The important part of this is not that seawater is good for feathers. The important part is the thing that inspired the research. The man who did it says he read that drinking seawater is good for people's hair, so he figured if it was good for hair, it would be good for feathers.

It is inspiring to watch the working of the scientific mind, to see the leap of logic that enabled our researcher to spring from follicles to feathers. It is touching, how our scientist took this information and used it to help make life cozy and warm for poultry. I don't know the research associate who did this, but I suspect he's got a full head of hair. There are people in this world who might think he had the most important part right there in front of him and ignored it in favor of the chickens. If seawater is good for people's hair, why aren't they doing research with people?

Have you noticed your forehead getting higher these days? Does it take you a lot less time to get a haircut than it used to? Is there more hair on your brush than there is on your head? What are you more concerned about, bald chickens or bald you?

Do you know how long people have been trying to figure out how to keep their hair? Probably since Eve told Adam, "You're getting a little thin on top, honey." Do you realize what an antidote for baldness would be worth? And they are doing research to help chickens?

Now before you run out to the car and head for the beach so you can guzzle down the incoming tide, there's a couple of things you need to know. First, seawater tastes awful, and second, drinking too much of it can poison you. Besides, I don't know for sure if it really does make your hair grow stronger. All I know is, there is a golden opportunity here for somebody to find out. Sometimes scientists just completely bewilder me.

# ANYTHING
# WORTH DOING
# IS WORTH
# OVERDOING

# BASEBALL

You would think that two out of three would be good enough. Everybody knows that nothing is more American than baseball, hot dogs, and apple pie. I'm real fond of hot dogs and apple pie. It's baseball I don't care anything about. I don't dislike baseball. It just doesn't matter to me if it's there or not. This is the sort of thing that makes folks look at you funny and accuse you of being a communist.

To be an American you are supposed to know what is going on out at the old ball game. You've seen all those World War II movies where to get back across the American lines, you had to tell the guard who won the World Series that year. If you didn't know, the guard figured you were a German and shot you. I'd be a goner. I can't tell you who won the World Series in World War II. I don't even know who won it this year. I don't care who won.

I don't care about any of the rest of the game either. People who are really interested in baseball are crazy about keeping statistics. This works out fine because at the baseball game you have plenty of time to figure out batting averages and earned run averages, and who holds the record for most stolen third bases by a left-handed shortstop. I suspect that a lot of the other people who go to baseball games just do it to get out of the house and sit around and drink beer in the bleachers.

You don't really have to pay attention to the game

137

because most of the time, nothing is going on. Of the eighteen people directly involved in a baseball game, the only three players doing anything on a regular basis are the pitcher and the catcher and the batter. Eight of the other fifteen people are sitting down in the dugout, and seven are standing around by themselves in the field. And everybody is waiting for something to happen.

I think that is why they call baseball The Great American Pastime. Everybody at the game has to find some sort of amusement to pass the time until some action breaks out. This is fairly easy for the fans in the bleachers. They can sit there with their scorecards and figure out what right-handed third baseman of Hungarian origin had the most runs batted in in the National League in 1937—and they can drink beer.

The players out in the field don't have it so good. They have to stand there for three outs before they get to sit down, and they have to remember what is happening just in case somebody hits the ball towards them and they have to do something about it. This discourages sleeping and reading books. Unfortunately it doesn't discourage spitting. So that's what they do. The great pastime of the Great American Pastime is spitting.

Everybody in baseball spits, and chews tobacco to provide themselves with a steady supply of ammunition. The players, the coaches—everybody. They stand around out there with a wad of tobacco crammed in their jaws, and they spit.

They don't spit in other sports. You don't see anybody spitting in football, or basketball, or golf, or tennis. They don't spit in ice hockey. They fight a lot in ice hockey, but they don't spit. Only in baseball. If it hadn't been for this spitting business, things could have turned out a whole lot different for me.

138

I decided at the age of twelve that I would give up my budding career as a concert pianist to become a major league baseball player. This came as a great shock to my mother and an unspeakable relief to my piano teacher.

Armed with resolve, a glove, and youthful enthusiasm, not to mention a lot of ignorance, I marched off to the Baker Village recreation center in Columbus, Georgia, a place where I figured some day they'd put up a brass marker saying, "This is the place where LeRoy Powell started his baseball career." I didn't know at the time that it was also the place where LeRoy Powell would end his baseball career.

Sixty or seventy of us future all-stars were there, trying out for little league, and half a dozen coaches were shrewdly eyeing us for places on their starting lineups. First we took turns in the outfield where a coach would hit the ball in our direction. Coolly, nonchalantly, with the athletic grace of a veteran, I positioned myself in center field. Finally, with a sharp report, the ball left the bat and arced long and high, heading my way. Carefully gauging the flight of the ball, I drifted back, then left, then right. "I've got it! I've got it," I yelled. It started down. I braced for action. The ball was getting nearer, nearer, spinning my way. I put my glove up. SPLAT! I had it! Glory! For a split second...until I tripped over my feet and fell backwards, and the ball rolled off loose like an accusation.

I slunk back to the bench, trying to kick up enough dust with my PF Flyers to provide a smokescreen from the gimlet eyes of the coaches. I could just see them, marking by my name, "no field." Well, no matter. I'd show them when the time came for batting practice.

The time came. We straggled into a ragged line, waiting our chance to knock the cover off the ball. I would like to tell you that when I stepped to the plate, I put one over the fence and into the street, and that the coaches fought among themselves to have me on their team. I'd like to tell you that, but it didn't happen. I was standing four or five batters from the front of the line when the kid ahead of me turned around. He was a tow-headed ruffian about as high as my shoulder. He looked me square in the eye, then lowered his head and spit on my foot.

Things like that can have a lasting effect on you. It was suddenly crystal clear that there was no way I could win in this situation. If I punched the kid in the snout for spitting on my foot, he would probably hit me back, and we'd have a fight on our hands. If I beat him up, I would have beat up somebody smaller than me and been a bully. If he beat me up, I would have lost a fight to a little kid, and I'd be a wimp. So I just stood there. I don't know how I did at batting. All I knew was this was a place I didn't want to be. Ever since then I can't go to a ball game without thinking that out there on the field somewhere is that kid. And he wants to come up in the stands and spit on my foot again.

I might have been a great baseball player. I may have developed a lifelong love for the game if when I was twelve that kid hadn't spit on my foot. You never expect the things that alter your dreams.

DRIBBLE

# DRIBBLE

Some things are right,
and some things are
wrong. Dribbling is one of
the wrong things. I think
basketball should be
changed so we don't have
dribbling anymore. I mean
the word "dribbling" should
be changed. It doesn't fit
the game.

Basketball is an excit-
ing, fast, and dramatic
game, and "dribble" is a
dumb-sounding word. You
get the ball from one end of
the court to the other by
dribbling it. Dribbledrib-
bledribble. It sounds idi-
otic.

We're dealing with a
great game played by su-
per-duper athletes, who
are forced to dribble. I
don't have any problem
with them bouncing the
ball up and down to move
it if it could be called something that fit instead of a

word that is associated with mindless drooling. A seven-foot tall man should not have to dribble. It's undignified. They dribble down the court, they dribble behind their backs, they dribble between their legs. There's even a foul for double dribbling. If I stood seven feet tall, I wouldn't put up with it.

The terms used in a sport should reflect the character of the game. "Slam dunk" sounds like basketball, so does "fade-away jump shot." Maybe dribble sounded good to James A. Naismith when he nailed a peach basket to the gymnasium wall in Springfield, Massachusetts and invented the game in 1891, but it's not the same game it was then. It has been refined on the playgrounds of America, honed to a contest that calls for a keen eye, quick reflexes and the stamina of a bulldog—a tall bulldog. Nowhere in the game as it is played today does it call for dribbling. Dribble sounds like you dropped the ball.

I think they ought to call it doobadooba. That is something that sounds like what's going on. When you bounce a basketball off the floor, it goes, dooba, dooba, dooba, dooba. Doesn't it make sense to call it what it is? You can doobadooba fast, and doobadooba slow. You can even just dooba.

Everything changes with the times, even sport. Basketball will be better off when we stop dribbling and start doobadoobing. It's time we put some new bounce in the old game.

# Deus Ex Machina or Murphy Was an Optimist

I swear. I'm not proud of it, but I do. This is not something that I do all the time. When every other word you use is a cussword, you lose cussing as a useful tool. I prefer to be selective about the occasions that I say "heck" and "darn" and "phooey." When you operate that way, the object of your cussing knows that it is getting special attention.

Take for instance the times when you as a consenting adult are dealing with a non-consenting piece of machinery. If it's busted, fix it. If you can't fix it, cuss it.

There is a widely held belief that machines are not alive. Those who adhere to this belief are people whose idea of what to do when the electric toaster malfunctions is to go to the store and buy a new toaster.

Those of us who resort to repairing things ourselves know differently. Of course machines are alive. And they've got a malevolent intelligence that they use to torment the humans around them. You can't trust a machine just because it has an innocent look on its face. It may sit around for years doing exactly what it's supposed to do, but behind that smoothly operating exterior, it's biding its time while it thinks of ways to drive you crazy.

That's why the toaster decides to go on the blink at the worst possible moment. It knows you have an important meeting that morning, so it holds your bread slices hostage and toasts them until they are

143

nothing but smoking cinders. It does this to get your day off to a lousy start so you'll go into your meeting with a bad attitude. It enjoys doing this.

Only a coward would let a machine pull a stunt like that without retaliating. When you get home that afternoon, you grab the toaster and proceed to the torture chamber—your work-shop. Out come the pliers. Out comes the screwdriver! Mwa-haha! The toaster cringes in fear as you unscrew its screws and remove its cover, exposing its vital innards to your evil gaze.

You are going to fix the toaster. It doesn't matter that you have never tried to fix a toaster before. By the time you are through with it, your toaster will be good as new, maybe better. It may set world records for toasting when you are done tuning it up. Happily, you set to work. In only a couple of hours you convert a defective appliance that burns toast into something that will never burn toast again—or toast toast for that matter.

In the process of transforming a machine from broken to destroyed, you have a real fight on your hands. Here you are, with every intention of returning the malfunctioning item to glowing good health, and your patient resists you every step of the way. When you and I get sick, we want to get well. Sick machines don't. They want to make you sick too, or injured, or crazy. This is the sort of thing that makes you turn the air in your vicinity a lovely shade of blue.

For some reason, machines are fond of people who actually do know how to fix them. That is why, when your car starts going clunkaclunkaclunka, and you take it to the mechanic, it doesn't go clunkaclunka for him. The very same automobile that was hardly able to drag itself to the garage suddenly sounds like it's ready to win the Indianapolis 500. You have to stand there and tell a greasy man holding a wrench, "It goes clunkaclunkaclunka."

Your car likes the mechanic. And it likes to see you standing there making foolish noises.

You can avoid this by doing your own auto repair. That's what your car wanted you to do in the first place. Once it gets you with a screwdriver in your hand, it's got you at its mercy.

It would be a lot easier if the things we were taught in school turned out to be true. Remember in history the part about how interchangeable parts revolutionized industry? I think it was Samuel Colt who came up with the idea that if he made all the parts in one gun like all the parts in the next gun, he could

145

make the guns faster and cheaper and when it came time to repair the gun, it would be easy. Just stick in a new standard part.

Remember how Henry Ford introduced manufacture by assembly line? The car moved along a track, and the workers stuck the same standard piece in the same standard place, and all the cars came out the same. Don't you wonder what happened to all that?

If everything is made of interchangeable parts, how come nothing you own uses them? When you bought your car, you figured you were getting a standard car with regular standard car parts. The only problem is, none of the standard parts ever break. This is something you find out when you go to the auto parts store. Let's say your fan belt breaks. Fan belts are a pretty standard item, or so it would appear to the casual observer. You stroll up to the parts counter and tell the man, "I need a new fan belt."

"What kind of car?"

"Ferdmobile Weasel."

"What year?"

"1987."

"V-8 or six cylinder?"

"Six."

"Automatic or manual transmission?"

"Automatic."

"Tinted windows or clear?"

"Clear."

"Air conditioner belt, water pump belt, or power steering belt?"

All you want is a new fan belt, but after you go through this litany of information, the parts clerk informs you they don't have one to fit your car because it's a special fan belt they only put on two cars, yours and another fool's. And his is broken too. And the factory in Albania that makes that particular belt was de-

146

stroyed in the big earthquake.

This forces you into creative repair. You take a part that doesn't belong there and try to make it fit. The joy in this is it makes your car even more a special case than it was when you started. Once you've figured out how to get a Muskrat fan belt on your Weasel by bolting a '52 Nash idler arm to the firewall and re-routing all the wires, hoses and cables to make it fit, you have made it unlikely that even somebody who knows what they're doing will be able to figure out how it's supposed to be. And since it's got all sorts of strange parts on it, it works differently from other cars, so you are the only one who knows how to get it to operate at all. This means you can never unload it. It's hard to sell a car whose air conditioner sucks instead of blows.

Some people don't have problems like this. They live in a charmed world where everything fits, where a standard part is a standard part, where when something breaks, there's a warehouse full of pieces to fix it.

It's just you and I who go through life with hybrid machines. We should be proud that we own things that are uniquely ours. I don't think this is what Sam Colt and Henry Ford had in mind, but it's exactly the sort of thing your car was plotting all along.

A car will wait for an opportunity to get you. It will sit there patiently while you take it all the way apart and put it all the way back together, and then it will show you the pieces you left out. A car will strip a thread on the last bolt. A car will send you to the auto parts store three times for every repair job you do on it. The first time you go to get the repair part. An hour later, you have to go back to get the repair part in the correct size. Two hours after that, you're there again to replace the repair part that you just broke.

147

If you think machines aren't alive, you've never tried to fix one. You have never offered your knuckles as a human sacrifice to a water pump. You have never grabbed a hot exhaust manifold with your bare hand. You have never checked every electrical circuit on a washing machine before you discover it's not plugged in. That's where cussing comes in. You swear at machinery because that's the only way you can get it to listen to you. If cussing doesn't get its attention, hit it with something.

# FISHING SHOWS

Have you ever been looking for something good on the TV on the weekend and come across a Famous Fisherman fishing show? The kind of program where Famous Fishermen travel all over the country to catch all kinds of fish. They go to big lakes like Toledo Bend in Texas or Okeechobee in Florida and catch large-mouth bass. They go to Lake Erie and catch walleye. They catch steelhead trout in the Columbia River, bonefish in the Florida Keys, and blue marlin in the Pacific Ocean. Everywhere they go, they catch fish.

It's amazing. And they catch something every third cast. Big fish. Giants. Just picture our hero, we'll call him Rolando, standing there on the deck of his supersonic bass boat, chunking that lure out there and jabbering away to the TV audience. One chunk, two chunks, three chunks...WHAMMO! Big fish!

I'd like to catch a big fish every third cast. I'd like to catch a big fish every three-thousandth cast. It's all I can do just to find the little ones now and then, and that's when I'm fishing on my personal favorite pond where I know every stump and snag. Famous Fisher-men go to uncharted waters, places they've never seen before, and three casts later they've got Moby Bass on the line.

I want to make it clear at this point that I do not go fishing merely to catch fish. I enjoy communing with nature, becoming a part of the world outdoors, becoming one with the environment. I enjoy watching the sun rise in the sky, a hawk circle near the clouds, a kingfisher swoop in along the bank, a squirrel scam-

per through the trees. Catching a fish is merely a
bonus. The outdoor experience is the real appeal.

You know if I'll tell you that, I'll lie to you about
other things, too.

Of course I want to catch fish when I fish. That's what I've got a tacklebox full of lures for. I know these lures catch fish. Rolando catches fish with them on TV...I've seen it. And I know there are big fish where the Famous Fishermen fish, because when they catch a big one, they throw it back. I swear. Rolando will drag in a ten pound largemouth bass, and lift it out of the water, and say, "Oooooweeee! That's a nice one!" It is not a nice one, it's a monster. Ninety-nine percent of the fishermen in the world have never caught a bass that size. Ninety-nine percent of those, if they did catch it, would take it to the taxidermist to get it stuffed so they could hang it on the wall. But what does Rolando do with it? He puts it back in the lake.

You know what I think? I think they're using professional fish. Those fish get paid to be on the Famous Fishermen shows. They are athletes, like professional football players and professional wrestlers. These fish do a lot of weightlifting and exercise until they get big and strong, and they turn pro and sign contracts to appear on the Famous Fishermen shows. And when they're not out in the lake being caught on TV, they all drive around in a Finnebago, smoking cigars and playing gin rummy. They just drive from lake to lake and get caught every week. That way, the Famous Fishermen can always catch a big one every third cast. It also explains why they always throw the big ones back. It's in the contract of the Fish Actors Gill.

This may also explain why you and I can fish all day and not catch anything worth lying about. All the big fish have turned pro and gone on television. I don't know about you, but I'm going to start watching those shows more carefully and see if I recognize any familiar faces.

152

# FINS AND SCALES
# AND FISHING TALES

There are two kinds of fishermen...People who catch fish and philosophers. The truth does not reside with either kind.

People who catch fish lie about the size of the fish they caught. There is a reason for that. I didn't know it until I caught a fish myself one day.

I was fishing in the Little Tennessee River near Dillard, Georgia. It was just me and the stream and the morning because the rest of my fishing buddies were still asleep at the motel. Carefully, I cast a tiny spinning lure toward a pile of brush at the edge of the stream. WHAMMO! I'm hit! Skillfully I maneuver the fish as he fights for his freedom. Finally, he surrenders. I have him. A nice 14-inch rainbow trout. To lots of people, that's not much of a fish, but to somebody like me, used to catching little or nothing, he was a giant. Then I did something I never thought I'd do. I put the fish back in the water and watched him swim away.

I was feeling pretty proud of catching the fish, and even more noble for letting him go, and I could hardly wait to find somebody to tell about it. I hurried back to the motel, and found my friends drinking coffee and bragging about fishing and women and other things they don't know anything about, and I told them the saga of me and my trout...and they didn't believe me. Here I'd caught and released this 20-inch rainbow, and they thought I was lying about it. That hurt. After my titanic struggle to land this three-foot monster, my friends acted like I made up the whole story.

This is what you get for doing something decent and sporting. I catch this fish that must have weighed, oh, 45 or 50 pounds, and turn it loose, and nobody thinks I'm telling the truth. If they hadn't stayed up half the night playing poker, they could have been there to see the fight for themselves. This trout, so long that it couldn't turn around in the stream, surely would have set a new world's record. An eight foot rainbow trout, and I, master angler and consummate sportsman, set it free. Honest.

You may have noticed that the fish grew a little bit since I caught him. As long as people think you're a liar anyway, why hold back and tell a little one—it's like my Daddy told me, "If you're going to do something, do it the best you can." People expect lies from fishermen, so the fishermen do their best to oblige.

That takes care of people who do catch fish. Most of us are the other kind...philosophers.

Philosophers will tell you that they are out there to enjoy the solitude and beauty of nature, and that it doesn't matter if they catch anything. This proves you don't have to catch fish to tell lies.

It is true that you can go fishing and not catch anything, just like it is true that your wife can go shopping and not buy anything. But your wife would be a lot happier if she spent some money, and you'd be happier if you caught some fish.

Well, I for one am tired of being a philosopher. I don't know about you, but I want to lie about something other than how much fun it is to sit in a boat all day getting sunburnt and bug bit and not having anything to show for it. I want to catch some fish like other folks do. The only difference between them and us is they catch fish and we don't. They've got a boat,

154

and we've got a boat. They fish in the lake and we fish in the lake. They've got lures and we've got lures. All this equipment will do everything...except help me catch fish. I would just as soon that situation came to an end. I figure those other guys have discovered a secret we don't know about.

I've given this matter a lot of thought. When you aren't catching fish, you've got plenty of time for thinking, and I believe I've got it. The other guys know when the fish are biting.

All this time we've thought it was their fancy boats and that sonar they've got, and those famous lures...It doesn't matter, folks. The only difference between a liar who doesn't catch fish and one who does is the one who does knows the secret of when to go.

Now you may have your own ideas about the best time to catch fish. You might think the phase of the moon has some effect on it, or the passage of weather fronts, or whether it's hot or cold or wet or dry, or if the water's clear or muddy. Those things don't have a thing to do with it.

The answer is so simple. The guy that runs the bait store has been telling us for years, but we haven't been listening.

Now think about it. When did the bait store proprietor say it was that the little bitty boy had a whole stringer full that was so heavy he couldn't lift them? When did the guy come in with the five fish that weighed 45 pounds? When were they really biting? When should you have been here? You know it, and so do I. The best time to fish is.......tadaaaaaaaaa ......last week!

I just want you to know there is never a charge for this valuable information.

# TACKLEBOX

I've got to get a new tacklebox. My old one isn't worn out—you don't wear out tackleboxes. You fill them up. My problem is, I believe in fishing lures.

I'll tell you something about fishing lures. There used to be a congressman from Georgia named Maston O'Neal who said, "If one damn fool can think something up, another damn fool will try it." Now that, folks, is the basis of the fishing lure industry. There's nothing you can think up lure-wise that some other fool won't try.

There are big lures, and little lures, and pretty lures, and ugly lures, and lures that look like a three-day hangover. There are fishy-looking lures, and froggy-looking lures, and mousy-looking lures, and worms...well, I don't even want to think about how many worms there are.

I must have a bushel of plastic worms. Plastic worms come in an appetizing variety of sizes and shades. You can get teeny weeny ones all the way up to great old big ones ten inches long or more. They come in every color you ever imagined, and a lot you didn't. I've got blue ones and purple ones and red ones and pumpkinseed colored ones that look like dirt sprinkled with pepper, and clear ones with sparklies in them, and watermelon-colored ones that look green like the outside of a watermelon, not red, like the inside of it. These different colors are supposed to match the disposition of the fish on a given day.

Do you remember mood rings? Back in the 1970's people bought mood rings that changed color from blue to purple to red, depending on your outlook while you were wearing them. I think it's supposed to be the same idea with colored worms, except you've got to guess what sort of mood the fish is in. If you get it right, the theory goes, the color will drive the fish crazy, and he won't be able to keep himself from attacking your worm. That's the theory. But I've never seen a fish that looked like he belonged in an asylum, so I don't know if it really works. I don't know if curly tailed worms really work, or straight tails, or blackberry flavored, or salt flavored. I just keep buying more worms.

The point is, there are lures in my tacklebox that ought to appeal to a fish, no matter what mood he's in.

I have got one called a Creek Chub Broken Back Fantail Shiner. It's special. On June 2, 1932, a young man named George Perry was fishing with a Creek

Chub Broken Back Fantail Shiner in a South Georgia oxbow called Montgomery Lake. He caught a 22-pound, 4-ounce largemouth bass. It's a world record that has lasted better than fifty years.

I've never caught a thing with my Creek Chub Broken Back Fantail Shiner. I've never caught a thing on lots of my lures. I've got some my father gave me that must be from the 1920's. I know I haven't caught anything with those, and I wouldn't be surprised to find out that old Dad didn't catch anything with them either.

As a matter of fact, in about forty years of fishing, I'll bet I have caught fish on no more than ten different kinds of lures. But I keep on buying new ones and filling up more tackleboxes.

If you aren't a fisherman, you may be saying, "LeRoy, you fool, if you aren't catching fish on these lures throw them away." If you were an old maid, would you throw away your hope chest? A tacklebox is not filled just with pieces of metal and wood and rubber and plastic. Somewhere, under a lilypad or beside a sunken log, lurks a giant fish. And at some point in his career, this fish wants to bite each lure in your box. If you're lucky he'll want to bite it when it's tied to your line.

Hope chest probably doesn't quite describe it. It's more like a ladies dresser. Drawers full of things to catch a big one. Women use jewels to get your attention. Fishermen use spinnerbaits. Women use Chanel No.5 and Givenchy perfume to drive you wild with desire. Fishermen use Doctor Juice and Fish Formula. It's all the same, just different fish. And just because these lures haven't caught anything yet doesn't mean they won't work someday.

It doesn't matter what you're fishing for. Lures aren't just fishbait, they're dreams...possibilities of

158

what might happen, if you're in the right place at the right time. And in case everything else fails, I've got a secret weapon. A man named Harry sent it to me. Yessir, folks, one of these days when I've thrown everything in the box at them and none of it has done any good, I've got a last resort to turn to—thanks to Harry. It's a little bitty kitchen sink. I'm going to have to try it. You never know what might work.

# THERE'S NO PLACE LIKE HOME...
## *Thank Goodness*

# THE LAWN

The lawn is the biggest idiot enterprise that was
nvented. Think about it. You pay good money for
eed, and good money for fertilizer. You put the
ed out, and you fertilize it, and you water it,
ut stuff on it to fight the bugs off. Then,
ass grows green and lush, you pay more
wn mower to go out and cut it down. If
the grass to grow tall, how come you
t in the first place? Because Mama

ens

nspiracy among grass seed grow-
urers, lawn mower manufactur-
lawn exists to keep you from
ld really enjoy, like fishing,
n the sofa, or any activity
n the yard, trying to per-

You
e dirt.
ything
have to
want to
yard, it
p by chig-
take your
go on, but

think up a lot of ex-
ith the grass in the

ia are lined with
n to Saint Ma-
and crimson
beautifying
e pleasant
Depart-
flowers
d is stop

ng you have
s the one who
ma. She'd get
room that she
d switches and
p that yard from

mowing the side of the road.

I told my wife that I want to start a Wildflowers in the Front Yard program. She won't let me do it. She's afraid that if I left the yard to take care of itself, I'd have lots of extra time.

Wives, for some reason, see time as something they have to fill up for you. The problem with this is that the things they dream up to occupy your time aren't the same as things that you'd think of. Mowing the lawn, or weeding it, or feeding it, or watering it aren't high on my list of leisure activities. Fishing is. But my bride never suggests that I should go fishing.

I've been thinking about this, and I believe the lawn is the place where the women's liberation movement started. This will come as a surprise to the younger among you, but there was a time, only [a] couple of generations ago, when most people did[n't] have lawns. What they had in their yards was di[rt]. And if any grass did decide to grow there, the chick[ens] would come along and peck it out.

There are lots of advantages to dirt yards. [You] don't have to water dirt. You don't have to fertiliz[e it]. You don't have to mow dirt. Dirt doesn't cost an[ything] to maintain. If there's a drought, you don't [have to] worry that your dirt will die on you. If you [want to] drive your car right out in the middle of th[e yard it] won't bother the dirt. You don't get eaten u[p by chig]gers in dirt. You can play marbles there, and [play with] toy cars and make roads and towns. I coul[d go on but] you get the idea.

Dirt is wonderful stuff. The only th[ing you had] to do to a dirt yard is sweep it. And who [do you think] used to sweep the dirt yard? Right. Ma[ma would be] out there in the yard with her brush b[room. It was] made by getting a lot of little limbs a[nd sticks and] tying them together. She would swee[p]

164

the road to the house, and it would be real pretty, because she would sweep nice curved patterns into the dirt.

That is the way it was before The Great Earline Uprising.

It was a fine spring day in Boaz, Alabama. The sun warmed the earth and hinted of summer to come. Earline Threadgill looked out the screen door at the yard. It was the middle of the morning, eight, or eight thirty, but already Earline had fired up the wood cookstove and fixed breakfast for Harold and the children, and washed the dishes and ironed a basket full of clothes and swept the house.

Now she stood, broom in hand, contemplating the yard. Out by the wood picket fence, the irises were blooming real pretty, and the boxwood looked nice lining the path to the front porch. But the rain last night had knocked a bunch of twigs and trash out of the big oak tree, and Earline faced the prospect of putting up her house broom and getting out the brush broom and tidying up the dirt yard.

At this point, Harold came sauntering around the house with a fishing pole in one hand and in the other, a can of worms he had dug up from the compost pile next to the barn. He intended to go to the creek and go fishing and catch up on a little sleep he had lost because he had been out all night in the rain on a coon hunt. Harold's life had, until that moment, been the carefree existence of a king in his castle. It was all going to change.

Earline pushed open the screen door, and raising her broom like a scepter yelled, "Whoa!" Harold whoaed. It was a turning point in history. There was steel in Earline's gaze and in her posture. Here was a peasant who finally realized that she had been doing all the work while the king lived a life of ease. The sunshine illumined her magnificent form as she stood, broom in hand, a living symbol of revolution.

"Harold," she said, "You turn yourself around this minute and put that fishing pole back in the shed. I want you to go down to that Feed and Seed Store, and I want you to get a sack full of fescue seeds and a sack of fertilizer, and a roll of chicken wire. I want you to get out there in that yard and plant that grass seed out in front of the house and put that fertilizer on it. And build a chicken coop to keep those hens in so they can't eat up those seeds or that grass. We are going to have a lawn. If I've got to spend all morning sweeping the inside of the house, I'm not spending all afternoon sweeping the outside of it too."

"And Harold, you might as well go to the hardware store and get a lawn mower, and cancel any plans you might have to go fishing—ever again."

Ever since The Great Earline Uprising we husbands have been stuck, prisoners of zoysia, in bondage to bermuda, captives of centipede. Like any other convict, we spend a lot of time trying to figure out ways of getting out. I even considered becoming a fruitarian.

The fruitarian movement started in California. Fruitarians believe that plants have feelings. I can understand how they could come to that conclusion. Don't willows weep, don't aspens quake, don't Susans get black-eyed? Plants are supposed to respond if you talk to them or play music for them. Would they do that if they didn't care?

Fruitarians are to the vegetable world what animal rights organizations are to the world of beasts. Fruitarians feel that we have been mistreating our plants, especially grass, and they want us to stop. They have even come out with a list of reasons why we shouldn't mow our lawns. I lost the list, but they had some dandy excuses.

166

One of them was that mowing grass wastes precious natural resources. Another was when you use a lawn mower, you hack up all sorts of innocent bugs and snails and things. That alone should get the animal lovers all fired up over this thing. But the biggest fruitarian concern was for the emotional well-being of the grass itself.

Actually, I don't know if it hurts grass to have its little blades sheared off or if it's more like a haircut. It could be that your lawn finds it embarrassing that you don't take it to a stylist for a razor cut or a perm or something.

The whole fruitarian business sounded a little strange to me, but I figured I could go along with just about anything that would get me out from behind the lawn mower.

You would think my bride would be good fruitarian material. When I was young and courting her, she seemed such a sweet thing, so sensitive to the feelings of every living creature. But after only twenty something years of marriage, she has developed an absolute indifference to the deeply rooted mental stress of the grass in her own yard. She doesn't care if the fescue is savagely cut down every time it reaches for the sun. I tried to raise her consciousness to all the anguish and pain. She looked me right in the eye and murmured three little words. "Mow the lawn."

# MALL MAZE

One of the major differences between men and women is that women will go to The Mall on purpose. Many of them will arrive before the doors open and not leave until closing time. They will spend all day cruising through the dress shops, prowling the racks, trying on dresses and skirts and slacks and blouses and listening to the saleslady telling them how darling they look in it all. They'll meet their friends there and attack the department stores and cookware stores and gift and gewgaw shops. I thought women do this because they love shopping at The Mall, but now I find out it's something altogether different. The reason they stay so long at The Mall is they can't find their way out.

This word comes to me from Mrs. Trimble, who called up and let me know what's going on. She sounded like somebody who knew what she was talking about.

According to the Trimble theory, the department stores at The Mall are designed like fish traps. It's easy to get in, but a booger to get out. This is the sort of thing that you ought to know about if it's true, so I went to my neighborhood mall and checked it out myself.

I'll admit that the only time I normally go to The Mall is when my wife takes me along as a beast of burden and credit card caddy, so being in unfamiliar territory by myself, I'd be bad to be lost anyhow. But

169

I think Mrs. Trimble may be on to something. It's simple to find a department store at The Mall. You just go to the end of The Mall, and there it is. Getting out once you've gotten in is not so easy.

It looked real pretty in there—all sorts of mirrors and mannequins and decorations—not to mention racks and racks of merchandise. I wandered in like Gretel's brother Hansel going into the gingerbread house. But when I was ready to leave, I discovered somebody had hidden the door. If the witch had been around, I'd have been cooked.

I remembered that I passed Perfumes and Cosmetics on the way in, so I headed to where I thought they were, but I ended up in Ladies Underwear instead. Everywhere I looked, there were mirrors and decorations and more mirrors. It was like a carnival fun house, but it wasn't fun. I noticed I couldn't see all the way across the store. There were partitions and potted plants and more mirrors in the way.

I was lost. Trapped like a rat in a maze of Fine China and Men's Shoes and Infant's Clothing. Through Furniture I roamed, past Misses Sportswear. I wanted my wife. I wanted Mrs. Trimble. I wanted my Mama.

I was standing in the middle of Housewares, tired and hungry and about to abandon hope when I felt it. A draft.

If you're lost in a cave you can follow a draft and find the entrance, so why not try the same thing in a store? With rekindled hope I headed into the faint trace of air, out of Housewares, through Rugs and Carpets, into Jewelry. And there I picked up the sweet smell of Perfume, followed it into Cosmetics, and I was saved. On the other side of a cart full of face powder was the door! You couldn't see it for the powder display.

Now why, you may ask, would a store want to get you lost? It's simple. What is a store there for in the first place? Right. To sell you things. It makes sense that the store can't sell you anything if you aren't in the store, and it makes even more sense that once they get you inside, it is to their advantage to keep you there. The more you search for a way out, the more things you see to buy. The longer they keep you the more they can sell you. It's as simple as that. They lure you into a maze of aisles and mirrors and merchandise and they've got you by the credit cards.

Now that Mrs. Trimble has let us in on this secret, we can go prepared. The next time you make an expedition to The Mall, take along a ball of twine and tie one end to the door when you go in. Unroll the ball as you go along. Then when you get ready to leave you can just wind yourself back to the entrance. If you don't have twine, you can find it in the stationery department—Stationery is in the middle of the store.

That takes care of the business about how come women stay so late at The Mall. I still don't know why they go there in the first place.

# Heel of the Loaf

I don't know if a tree falling in a deserted forest makes any sound. That sort of metaphysical stuff is fine for people who don't have anything more important to figure out. The thing I've been puzzling over is whether, when I am telling my family how wonderful the end pieces on a loaf of bread are, do I make a sound? I have lectured, reasoned, begged, and hollered on the end piece proposition, and my whole tribe just sits there and looks at me like I have been speaking to them in Swedish. And they ignore the end pieces on the bread, too.

Here we have a natural resource going to waste, and I seem to be the only one who cares. Don't end pieces deserve to be treated like other slices? Aren't they bread too, with all the feelings and hopes and aspirations of the rest of the loaf? But people call them heels, and leave them in the sack until they get stale and hard and moldy.

Think of the poor end piece, constantly passed over, watching while the other slices head merrily out to the toaster for breakfast, or to be anointed with mustard and pickles and bologna and taken out on picnics. Where is the end piece while all this is going on? Stuck in the bread sack, lonely, forlorn, unwanted, unloved.

If people would only open their minds and hearts to these outcastes of the food world, they would discover that they have been missing the benefits of a remarkable slice of bread. It is a well-known fact that the end piece is the most nutritious part of the loaf. There are more vitamins in the end piece. Because of its additional crust area, there is more fiber, too. The end piece is always brown, no matter what kind of loaf it's on, and everybody knows that brown bread is better for you than white bread. Dieters should note that end pieces are often thinner than the rest of the slices in the loaf. It makes sense then that the end piece would be less fattening.

Aside from the healthful benefits, the end piece has practical advantages over the rest of the loaf. If you have ever made a peanut butter and jelly sandwich with ordinary bread slices, you have experienced the misfortune of a glob of jelly falling through a hole in the bread and getting all over your hands or in your lap. Users of the end piece do not have to worry about something like that happening to them. There are no holes in an end piece. They are sturdier, too, so you can make a sandwich with a big slice of ripe home—grown tomato and feel confident that the middle of the bread is not going to go soggy and collapse on you halfway through eating it. And for finishing up a big plate of beef stew, nothing is better than an end slice of bread. It is strong enough to sop up the juice in the bottom of the plate without tearing apart, but absorbent enough to get every last drop.

And how about the status value. Bread comes in all sizes from super-duper giant sandwich loaves, down to little bitty ones that are a challenge to get much food on which makes them perfect for serving in a buffet at your party. But no matter what the size of the loaf, you never get more than two end pieces. The end pieces are the designer originals of breaddom. As rare as they are, you'd think people would fight to get them. Anybody can have regular bread. It takes a person with real fashion clout to get the end pieces.

And finally, my fellow Americans, this country was forged by hardy and resourceful men and women, who came to a wilderness and with grit and determination built a nation of condominiums and shopping malls. They didn't do it by throwing away valuable assets. Leaving the end pieces to wither and die in the pantry is un-American. It goes against all the things this country stands for, and it could lead to the downfall of civilization as we know it.

There. I've said it and I'm glad. I've used these arguments over and over on my family to a response of resounding apathy. You would think that reasoned, logical, patient explanation would work. We still have a pantry full of bread sacks with nothing in them but moldy end pieces. And so I wonder, when a father talks, does he make a sound? ...Hello?...Is anybody out there?

# RICH TRASH

I don't know why I get mail from the Solid Waste Council, but I do. They sent me the results of a study by Le Projet du Garbage. If I guess right, that means The Project of Garbage. I am not making this up. Le Projet du Garbage was a study done by the University of Arizona and the University of Wisconsin.

For two years, these researchers rooted around in the garbage cans of Milwaukee, Wisconsin. They were trying to find out what people throw away. Now I don't know how the folks in Milwaukee feel about his, but if I went out in the morning and found a bunch of college researchers going through my garbage can, I don't care if they were from Le Projet du Garbage, I think I'd show them Le Barrel du Shotgun. It's bad enough when dogs get in the trash, but at least the dogs don't go around telling everybody what was in there. The researchers did. Here's the hot news. Le Projet du Garbage found that rich people throw away less garbage than poor people.

This may have come as a revelation to the Solid Waste Council folks, but it's something I've suspected all along. How do you think rich people get to be rich?

Rich folks don't open a new bottle of catsup when they've already got a half full one on the pantry shelf. Rich folks don't take one bite out of an apple and leave it laying around on the coffee table. The rich don't leave the hot dogs unwrapped in the refrigerator until they turn dark and yurky looking. Rich people eat a whole loaf of bread before they start on a new loaf. Rich people even eat the end pieces. Rich people don't get rich by wasting stuff.

I have been telling my family this for years, and now there is solid support from the Solid Waste Council and Le Projet du Garbage.

The reason rich people stay rich is they close the top of the potato chip bag when they are through with it, instead of leaving it open where the chips can get stale and soggy. The reason we poor folks stay poor is we don't. We act like we've got money to throw away...and garbage to throw away, too.

I have told my family that, and they ignore me. I imagine they'll ignore Le Projet du Garbage. I don't know why I get mail from the Solid Waste Council.

# Pump Toothpaste

Every time you make progress in one direction, you lose ground in another one. Take for instance, the development of pump toothpaste.

Now a tube has been our standard dentifrice delivery device for years. There are two ways to get toothpaste out of the tube. Some people get it out of the middle, and some get it out of the end.

These people are known as gooshers and mashers, respectively. These people are also known as married couples, because they are always married to each other. Gooshers are people who take a casual view of the routine of dental hygiene. They grab the toothpaste by the middle of the tube and goosh it out on their toothbrushes. This method gives the toothpaste tube an hourglass figure with wrinkles all over it. Gooshers never put the top back on the tube, and they never put the tube away.

Mashers are fastidious types who approach tooth cleaning in a neat and methodical manner. They take the toothpaste tube and mash it from the bottom, carefully rolling the empty portion of the tube up behind them. This keeps the toothpaste compactly herded into one end of the tube. Mashers always put the top back on the tube, and put the tube away when they are through with it.

Gooshers always marry mashers. Mashers always marry gooshers. And for all these years, there have been toothpaste wars in the bathroom. Mashers, being tidy and methodical, think gooshers are slobs. Gooshers, being casual and easygoing, think mashers are nuts.

Now here comes science with the toothpaste pump. It's a hard plastic cylinder with a button on top. You can't goosh toothpaste out of its middle. You can't mash toothpaste out of its end and roll it up. You just push the button on the top, and out comes a perfect, measured, glop of toothpaste. It stays neat. It's wonderful.

No longer do you have to holler at your wife for leaving the top off the tube that she's mangled and left on the sink, where it can droob toothpaste down the side of the basin. No longer does she accuse you of having an unhealthy obsession with neatness, and besides who cares if the top's still on the tube or not. Serenity reigns in the bathroom, and sitting there waiting for its Nobel Peace Prize is the easy to use, tidy toothpaste pump.

Hooray for science. Technology has taken a grand leap forward. But it's not doing anything at all for the institution of marital discord. For all this time, whenever we needed to work up an argument, all we had to do was bring up the other partner's toothpaste etiquette. It was guaranteed to be good for a short but lively battle. Now that source of friction is gone. Gone with the tube.

That's not good, it's bad. All marriages need some fights, just like all stew needs some pepper. It adds a touch of spice that keeps things interesting. The trick is to keep the stew spicy without ruining it. When you don't have something trivial like toothpaste to argue over, you're liable to start slugging it out over important things.

I know the pump toothpaste people think they

have done a good thing by establishing peace and harmony in the bathroom, but they have forgotten that if you want to hold things together, you need a little friction.

Of course there's still the problem of who hogs all the covers on the bed, and who tries to sleep in the middle.

## Cal Warlick

Cal Warlick was born in Columbus, Georgia, and is presently Creative Director and editorial cartoonist for the *Gwinnett Daily News*, a newspaper owned by *The New York Times*. His varied art background includes experience in advertising, as a gag cartoonist, cartoon animator, illustrator and news art director with WAGA-TV, Atlanta's CBS affiliate. He has received numerous awards for his work, including eight Emmy awards from the Georgia chapter of the National Academy of Television Arts and Sciences. His illustrations and editorial cartoons have also been honored by the Broadcast Designers Association, Suburban Newspapers of America, and the Georgia Press Association.

## LeRoy Powell

LeRoy Powell was born in Opelika, Alabama, raised in Columbus, Georgia, graduated from the University of Georgia, and has been employed for 22 years with WAGA-TV, Atlanta's CBS affiliate. He has been honored twice by the journalism society Sigma Delta Chi with the Green Eyeshade Award for commentary. He has received 25 Emmys for commentary, writing, and entertainment specials from the Atlanta chapter of the National Academy of Television Arts and Sciences. And most recently the organization awarded him an Emmy for individual excellence in news writing.

LeRoy has been married to the same lady for over twenty years and has two children, one of each variety. He goes fishing when he can, eats barbeque when he can get it, jogs to lose weight and plays golf for aggravation. He also rides a motorcycle and generally has a good time wherever he is.